CONTEMPORARY
CRITICISM
OF LITERATURE

CONTEMPORARY CRITICISM

OF LITERATURE

BY

ORLO WILLIAMS

HASKELL HOUSE PUBLISHERS LTD.

Publishers of Scarce Scholarly Books

NEW YORK. N. Y. 10012

1971

First Published 1924

HASKELL HOUSE PUBLISHERS Ltd.
Publishers of Scarce Scholarly Books
280 LAFAYETTE STREET
NEW YORK, N. Y. 10012

Library of Congress Catalog Card Number: 73-155148

Standard Book Number 8383-1248-9

CONTENTS

Contents

type—but literary criticism not its most appropriate field—Mr. T. S. Eliot on the functions of criticism—the practical impulse—contemporary expressions of it.

IV

No authoritative figure of this type among present-day critics—the moralistic critics—Mr. Clutton Brock—Mr. Hugh Fausset—Mr. Middleton Murry.

V

The philosophical critic need not be romantic—Professor Santayana on Lucretius—Mr. T. S. Eliot's view of the subject matter of criticism—Mr. Lytton Strachey—Mr. T. S. Eliot—Mr. Percy Lubbock's "The Craft of Fiction."

VI

The aims and methods of practical criticism—its value and limitations—insularity of English criticism—Professor Saintsbury—Mr. John Bailey—Dr. Edmond Gosse—Mr. J. C. Squire—Mr. Robert Lynd.

VII

The future of literary art and criticism—the "three publics"—the conflict between "taste" and "life" accentuated to-day by the influence of the great reading public—the different state of affairs in France, Italy and other European countries—Latin "taste" preserved by the smallness of the reading public—the difficulties of English critics—the commercial standard—Mr. J. D. Beresford's preface—the duty of a critic—the importance of a critical background—criticism a necessary illumination.

PREFACE

My thanks are due to my friend, Mr. J. C. Squire, for suggesting to me the form which this book has taken. It is not a series of disconnected studies, but an endeavour to present a view of criticism and illustrate it from the work of some modern English critics. In the course of the book I have pointed out some faults of English criticism in general, which have been borne in on me, particularly, during periodical attempts to present current English literature to a foreign public in a foreign language. But I do not imagine myself exempt from any of these faults, or exceptionally furnished with any of the compensating virtues. Also, I have not been exhaustive, but on that head I am bound to plead that my space was strictly limited.

A large part of the first chapter appeared in the Literary Supplement of *The Times* to whose Editor I make all acknowledgments.

O. W.

August, 1924.

I

THE IDEAL OF CRITICISM.

EVERY critic, sooner or later, in one place or another, must come to discuss the nature of criticism ; and, possibly, the book now beginning might have been adequately composed, after sedulous searches and artful dovetailing, from the writings of the author's contemporaries. Yet it may be presumed that a topic so inevitable has a correspondingly inevitable interest, and that the spontaneous reflections of one more critic on the subject of his activity will in their turn find readers and critics, thus keeping alive a delightful discussion that will only end with the extinction of humanity.

All human beings are critics. Some are critics in general, others only of the particular : many are merely ejaculatory, and few have attained to the complete expression of their discriminations. The infant, as he clutches with tiny fingers one object after another, conveys these instinctively towards his mouth, for there, where his sense is keenest, is his seat of judgment. Here, in infancy, is the type of man's ancient activity, curiosity. Curiosity breeds criticism, for the productiveness of experiments depends upon the rejection of some results and the adoption of others. These rejections and adoptions, rudimentary though they may often be, combine into a system : the more active the mind, and the more relations into which it enters, the greater is the number of these individual systems. In a well-developed human being they are innumerable, relating to every sense and every kind of perception, from those of food and drink at one end of the scale to those of moral and intellectual quality at the other. They are all critical systems, and they have been formed by deliberately critical methods. It is, therefore, unnecessary for the critics of the arts to defend their activity, since it springs from the nature of mankind. A blind man might with some reason complain of those who persisted in seeing, but there could be no better example of logical inconsistency than that a man who professed, as many do, a nice taste in French cookery, or a woman who expressed herself critically on the methods of housewifery, should complain, when another gave his opinion in public upon poetry or painting, that this pronouncement was arrogant and uncalled for.

The professional critic of art and letters, who produces what is specifically called " criticism " to-day, is of a comparatively late emergence in human society. The demand for him created him, as it created many another tradesman of whom the more primitive races were in no need, and who would have found, had he existed in their day, no facilities for practising his profession. No mystery, then, enshrouds the origin of criticism—and for the purpose of this book, I must confine the meaning of this word mainly to the criticism of literature—since it was simply a specialisation of a human system of perceptions. Literature existed, people thought and talked about it, some more articulately and wisely than their fellows. The words of these were reproduced, and society found it worth while to pay—not very much—to read them. Far more recondite trades are to be found upon the lists of a modern Labour Exchange : the demand and the facilities which produced critics were broad and elementary. And, since the facilities have increased immeasurably and the critics multiplied accordingly, it may be deduced that the phenomenon was not unreasonable.

Organised criticism can never be independent of these two factors, demand and opportunity. It is the common cry of all conscientious critics that they are sorely felt limitations to expression, if not to the reflection which should precede it. Galled by their trammels, indeed, critics are apt to be contemptuous of them and to minimise their real importance. They would consider it, many of them, derogatory to their art to inquire what exactly was the demand and of what nature the facilities that immediately conditioned it. Yet those are functions of the age they live in, which it would be futile to ignore, even were it possible. These functions differ from age to age, and they are not without interest in themselves. In fact, though the aim of this book is to illustrate a general view of criticism by contemporary examples, I should hold it negligent not to give to these factors, demand and opportunity, an extended consideration : and this I leave to the following chapter where I shall inquire generally to what extent the literary fashion of the present time in England is a condition, limiting or otherwise, of criticism. From this inquiry, contemporary critisicm should emerge in a definite, practical shape and preserve a recognisable identity of feature for the remainder of the discussion. Those who are impatient of general considerations and wish to come immediately into contact with material facts may be invited to turn over a few pages at once and return, if they will, after finishing the book to the remainder of the present chapter. But I confess that, for the moment, I can postpone with an easy mind the discussion of the contemporary factors in criticism, in order to think of those elements in it which, like man's soul, are eternal or, at least, timeless, essential and universal. And perhaps it may not be a waste of time to reflect what in itself is this activity which generations mould into different shapes but which they never disintegrate, much less destroy.

Nobody but the prejudiced will deny that there is an ideal element in criticism, for what, indeed, is good criticism but a comparison of the actual with the ideal, of the particular poem with poetic beauty, of the particular picture with the ideal of form, and so forth ? But is there, to go further, an ideal of criticism with which particular criticism can be compared ? Had Plato been living to-day, he might well have composed a dialogue upon this thoroughly modern subject, for, on his own theory of the immortal forms of mundane things, he could hardly have refused to so frequent an activity as criticism an ideal counterpart in the realm of the eternal but intangible ideas. And even if all the inspired dialectic put into the mouth of Socrates had failed, in this instance, to reveal criticism in itself as a sufficiently pure essence, he would certainly not have failed to throw a considerable amount of light upon its nature. No time is better spent than in considering the possible answers to absolutely simple questions : and, if a modern Plato had imagined the meeting of a modern Socrates, let us say, in a wine vault off Fleet Street, with Doctor Edmund Gosse, Mr. J. C. Squire, Mr. Middleton Murry, Mr. John Bailey, Mr. T. S. Eliot, Professor Saintsbury and Mr. Percy Lubbock, no simpler and more searching question could well have been propounded over the first round of sandwiches than, " Is there a perfect criticism ? "

We have, unfortunately, lost the knack of philosophical dialogue, or at all events the love for it ; and, in the absence of a Plato, it would be unwise to attempt a dramatisation of the conflicting views that would arise upon a question which so nearly touched all these contemporary authorities. Yet we may ask the question none the less, and see what will come of it. Since any criticism is a more or less coherent system of discriminations, perceptions or judgments, relating to a specific object or class of objects, one of the first and most obvious remarks to be made is that it cannot occur *in vacuo*. Not only cannot nothing criticise nothing, but nothing cannot be criticised by anything or anybody. Criticism, that is, cannot exist apart from the object of criticism, and there is no such thing as " pure " criticism, in the sense of a purely self-sufficient, or self-supporting activity. Pure music, imagined as the pure music of the eternal spheres, is conceivable, but it would be difficult to imagine a heavenly motion or harmony that would give off pure criticism. And lest this particular remark should seem little more than an idle truism, with no real bearing on the subject-matter, it may be well to bring in reality with a quotation from Mr. T. S. Eliot's book, " The Sacred Wood," a small critical portmanteau admirably packed with controversial topics. Mr. Eliot, speaking of a French critic, M. Julien Benda, says :

" But what an advantage a man like

15

M. Benda has over Arnold. It is not simply that he has a critical tradition behind him, and that Arnold is using a language which constantly tempts the user away from dispassionate exposition into sarcasm and diatribe, a language less fitted for criticism than the English of the eighteenth century. It is that the follies and stupidities of the French, no matter how base, express themselves in the form of ideas . . . . A man of ideas needs ideas, or pseudo-ideas, to fight against. And Arnold lacked the active resistance which is necessary to keep a mind at its sharpest."

Putting aside for the moment Mr. Eliot's insistence here on the combative element in the critic's activity, his remark is an interesting and, in the main, just application of the essential fact that there can be no criticism in a vacuum. Even a partial vacuum, as he implies, is imperfect. Tea-leaves at the bottom of a pot without water do not produce tea : nor do facts without an infusion of ideas give rise to criticism. Undoubtedly English criticism may often be observed, if one may so put it, assiduously attempting to make tea without water ; but criticism is not entirely to blame if the result is unsatisfactory. As

a nation we abound in acts and are fruitful
in images, but it is with difficulty that we
formulate precise ideas : and those creative
writers who maintain that critics are a dull
race, deficient in understanding, might often
do worse than consider how far the want of
clarity and incisiveness in their own ideas has
hindered comprehension. For the critic must
try to focus his view and give an outline to the
vague : and if this outline be sometimes other
than that which the creator of the object of
criticism intended, it is he who is to blame
for imposing an unnecessary task upon the critic.

To return, however, to the fundamental
question—if criticism cannot exist in a vacuum,
it may be asked whether it can exist in completeness. Could there, in fact, be an absolute
criticism which should play a part in the sum
of things considered as an ideal whole ? For,
if not, we begin to see the essential limits of
criticism. There is a section of Professor
Croce's " Breviario di Estetica "—itself a
chapter in a profound book called " Nuovi
Saggi di Estetica " (New Essays on Aesthetics)
—which assists in answering this question.
In this section which is headed " Criticism
and the History of Art," one of the great
philosophical critics of our day develops

briefly but decisively his lofty view of the critic's function. He begins by giving full weight to the current criticisms of the critic, as tyrannous pedagogue, judge of already decided causes, or mere amiable museum-guide. There is truth in all these views, he says, for the pedagogue embodies experience, the judge stands for taste, and good interpretation rests upon knowledge. A critic must have these three things—artistic experience, taste and knowledge—yet these are only the antecedents of criticism. By their help the critic does no more than fulfil his primary duty, to place himself at the artist's point of view. His own specific contribution is that of thought, by which alone he comes, even if he be an artist himself, to full consciousness of art. Criticism, in Signor Croce's eyes, is neither a swoon of ecstasy, nor a religious exercise, nor a mortification of the spirit, still less a grubbing up of irrelevances : it is the live work of a live mind. There is only one art and one criticism alone, in the profoundest and widest sense. The aim of criticism is aesthetic, the determination and elucidation, that is, of the beautiful, but its result is history, for it is the full account of an artistic fact. " The true and complete criticism," he says—and it is the reply to all those who ignorantly accuse him of basing criticism upon an arbitrary basis of abstract logic—" is the serene historical narration of that which has happened."

If this view be a true one, it follows that in the absolute or sum of things criticism must be transformed : like Bottom, the weaver, it must be translated from its sublunary appearance. And the transformation can be regarded in two ways, which are complementary, according as the universe is considered in its static or its dynamic aspect. If it be considered as above and beyond time, to imagine it as being at rest is an approximation to the truth. The " energy of no motion " was Aristotle's term for the supreme contemplation of eternal verities. In this aspect of the universe criticism, like every other activity, must appear to be complete, that is, to have attained its end. There is no longer any distinction between past, present and future : all is one. All that has happened and all that ever will happen has happened, and the serene narration of it is accomplished too. Criticism exists, because nothing has ceased to exist, but it has now become co-extensive with its object, and all the conflict of imperfection has disappeared. The thing created and the thing criticised are one. To regard the other aspect of the sum of things leads to the same result. Of a universe in eternal motion, eternally developing in conformity with an eternal but self-imposed law, there could only be one adequate critic ; for where could the experience and the knowledge be and from whence could the thought be added to these but in and from the eternal Magnitude itself ? "God saw everything that He had made and behold it was very good," wrote the Hebrew narrator of the Creation. Absolute criticism could only be such a self-reflection, an autonomous complement of creation, from which hardly eternal subtlety could distinguish it. God alone can criticise Himself, and that is why the speeches of Lucifer in "Paradise Lost," for all their dramatic power, and those of Mephistopheles in the Introduction to Goethe's "Faust," for all their irony, are fundamentally unsatisfactory. They are merely idealisations of human, imperfect criticism, bound to disappear like all other imperfect manifestations in the perfect wholeness of the eternal Whole.

Absolute criticism, then, is no more within our power of comprehension than God Himself : as a possibility we can conceive it, but, sublimate and refine as we may our own human idea of criticism, we can find no image for it. Yet, from this short excursion into the realm of ideas, things become apparent which are not at all beside our mark. One of these is that, if we regard the activity of criticism rather than its aim, the nearest possible approach to the ideal criticism in our world of appearances appears to be the criticism exercised by an artist upon his own work. Here, though imperfectly and with a variable approximation to completeness, criticism is fused with its object, and its aim—whether it be conceived as serene narration, elucidation or simply as judgment—is fulfilled. The steps in the process are hidden, it is true, at least until some historian unearths the poet's rough copies : but if, in these cases, the actual utterances of criticism are not revealed, their effect is there in the work of art itself ; whereas, unhappily, in the more ordinary kind of human criticism, where one mind reflects upon another for the benefit of others still, the difficulty of observing any effect at all is extreme. Indeed, even the best of critics might legitimately lament that he and all his kind were Cassandras *à rebours*, condemned to tell their fellows what actually had occurred and to persuade none of their veracity. The blending of the creative and the critical faculties—a process more complete, for example, in a Baudelaire than a Swinburne—is a truly happy occurrence and is present to some extent in all genuine artistic creation. Mr. T. S. Eliot, in his article on "The Function of Criticism," which appeared in *The Criterion* for October, 1923, made the same point when he wrote :

"Matthew Arnold distinguishes far too bluntly, it seems to me, between the two activities : he overlooks the capital importance of criticism in the work of creation itself. Probably, indeed, the larger part of the labour of an author in composing his work is critical labour ; the labour of sifting, combining, constructing, expunging, correcting, testing : this frightful toil is as much critical as creative. I maintain even that the criticism employed by a trained and skilled writer on his own work is the most vital, the highest kind of criticism ; and (as I think I have said before) that some creative writers are superior to others solely because their critical faculty is superior. There is a tendency, and I think it is a whiggery tendency, to decry the critical toil of the artist ;

to propound the thesis that the great artist is an unconscious artist, unconsciously inscribing on his banner the words Muddle Through."

Mr. Eliot admitted at the same time that the discrimination which comes so hardly to some writers has " in more fortunate men flashed in the very heat of creation." Where the creation is very great, such a flash must be, humanly speaking, perfect criticism, but, by its very nature, it must be individual, transitory and barely articulate : like the electric spark that in a chemical experiment combines two gases to form water, its effect is only the testimony to its existence.

Criticism, in its more general sense, cannot be of this kind. It is too pure an essence, too white a light, for average human minds ; and it presumes that mystery, of which we still have no adequate notion, the action of a mind upon itself. Criticism, as we usually understand it, is the action of one mind upon the work of others ; and it is clear, if we reflect upon the ideal criticism, how imperfect this action must inevitably be.

Yet this does not imply that the greatest artist is the greatest critic, or that any artist is necessarily a good critic, as many artists would like to suppose. The germ of ideal criticism does not always lurk in the purely artistic sensibility, though we may agree with Mr. Eliot that, " as sensibility is rare, unpopular and desirable, it is to be expected that the critic and the creative artist should frequently be the same person." To criticise the work of other minds with authority necessitates some addition to the artistic equipment besides the power of automatic or even deliberate self-criticism : so that, in another sentence in his article just quoted, Mr. Eliot seems to be tilting a little unjustly at Mr. Middleton Murry when he accuses him by implication of the " whiggery tendency " to think that the great artist is the unconscious artist. In his fascinating lectures on " The Problem of Style," Mr. Murry has made it perfectly clear that he holds no such view : but what he does say with justice in his "Aspects of Literature " is that " the poet who would be a critic has to make his philosophy conscious to himself ; to him as a poet it may be unconscious." If we substitute the words " only subconscious " for " unconscious " the judgment is, perhaps, more exact, but we add little to its truth. Criticism in general is throughout a fully conscious activity : it is a human intellectual process, attended by all the possible virtues and defects of the human intellect.

This is another cardinal fact which becomes apparent when contemplating the ideal of perfect criticism : an adequate notion of criticism must recognise the necessity of both these qualities, the human and the intellectual. But there is a side-issue which, by the reader's leave, it is now convenient to clear out of the way. In modern times it has been asserted that there is a kind of criticism called " creative " criticism which, by some mysterious virtue in its author, avoids the more obvious imperfections of ordinary criticism ; and those who assert it appeal to the very truth which emerged from the question whether there was a perfect type of criticism, namely that the ideal type of criticism is that which is fused in creation. But the assertion rests upon a false analogy : creative criticism is not analogous to critical creation. Mr. Eliot, again, in his article on " The Function of Criticism" puts the case with admirable brevity :

" If so large a part of creation is really criticism, is not a large part of what is called ' critical writing ' really creative ? If so, is there not creative criticism in the ordinary sense ? The answer seems to be that there is no equation. I have assumed as axiomatic that creation, the work of art, is autonomous ; and that criticism, by definition, is *about* something other than itself. Hence you cannot fuse creation with criticism as you can fuse criticism with creation. The critical activity finds its highest, its true fulfilment in a kind of union with creation in the labour of the artist."

Further, since this assertion is most frequently made on behalf of impressionistic critics—those who aim at interpreting a work of art through their own personal impressions of it—its denial is reinforced by a remark of the same author's in the " Sacred Wood " :

" So far as you can isolate the ' impression,' the pure feeling, it is, of course, neither true nor false. The point is that you never rest at the pure feeling ; you react in one of two ways, or . . . . in a mixture of the two ways. The moment you try to put the impressions into words, you either begin to analyse and construct, to ' ériger en lois,' or you begin to create something else."

That *is* the point : the critic in his writing, and just in the degree that he strives for style in its proper sense, inevitably creates " something else," but it is important that he should not deceive himself into supposing that he creates, or for any mind outside his own re-creates, the work of art which he is criticising. No two contemporary critics differ more fundamentally than do Mr. Eliot and Mr. Middleton Murry on the questions of the critic's function and the critical standard, yet on this point they are agreed, though they part company almost at the gate of agreement. And, if the former were to demur to the wording of the latter's statement in "A Critical Credo" ("Countries of the Mind") that the function of criticism is primarily to provide a means of self-expression for the critic, he would not object to the subsequent sentence : " The critic stands or falls by the stability of his truth, and necessarily by his skill in communicating his truth." Moreover, in his " Problem of Style," Mr. Middleton Murry, with all the tensity of conviction which is his peculiar quality, puts unexceptionably the limits and conditions within which a good critic can be considered creative :—

" . . . . the critic needs to have an apprehension of the unique and essential quality of his author ; he needs to have frequented him until he is saturated with his mode of experience. He is, in fact, in a position analogous to that of the great writer himself. He, in search of a plot, looks for an incident that shall be completely congruous to his harmonised experience of life ; the critic, in search of a quotation, looks for one that shall be completely congruous to his harmonised experience of the author's work. He has become—in all but name—a creative artist in miniature himself. He looks for some conjuncture, some incident in the work of a great writer, which was so precisely fitted to his complex mode of experience that it served in the office of a prism : through it the whole spectrum of his emotions is suddenly concentrated into a ray of intense pure light—a perfect condensation of the whole universe of experience into a dozen lines, or a hundred words."

This statement needs no gloss except to point out that it is one thing to select a prism from the artist's own work and another to use the critic's own personality, as the impressionist critics do, as a lens for the projection of that work upon public opinion.

This point having been disposed of, it remains to realise how much is implied in the recognition that criticism, as we only can know or practise it, is a human activity, and that as such, no matter with what gifts of expression, insight and intellectual power a critic be endowed, it must fall lamentably short of the ideal, the perfect criticism. Its perfection must be rooted in the imperfection of all things human, and among human perfections, at best, it must be of an order inferior to the highest. Critics, chastened from without by the indifference and contumely of their fellows, are obliged also to chasten themselves from within when they reflect upon their own activity : and this, perhaps, is a salutary dispensation, since criticism, in its efforts to attain truth, must strive to transcend its limitations, to stand above the temporary and the transitory, and to be—as a phrase of modern cant has it—" Olympian " in knowledge, if not in language. The good critic, thus, is always straining towards an unattainable ideal, nor does he forget so often as men suppose how unattainable it is. And it may be said that in our present age, the intensity of the striving and the consciousness of this disability have increased. The critical

commonplaces, the stereotyped literary
" qualities " and the formal rules which were
accepted by an age such as Dryden's gave the
critic sure weapons and limited his field of attack.
How far critical genius could enlarge those
limits Dryden proved, but of our modern
analytical uneasiness he displays no trace.
Then the path of criticism was mapped out :
now, if criticism is to be profound, it must
be a voyage into the unknown, for which general
taste supplies no map and common example
fixes no procedure. It is a remarkable
experience, exhilarating yet almost heart-
breaking, for a critic of to-day to observe with
what assurance and success Dr. Johnson in
his " Lives of the Poets " moves among the
" Topics " of criticism. He was not bothered
by the spectre of interpretation nor by the
impishly varying meaning of words. Every
epithet which he used in praise or blame then
had a meaning which men and women of taste
recognised.* They did not even start when
he said that the rustic images in " Lycidas "
were disgusting, for propriety was a perfectly
intelligible topic and the right views on it, at
the time, universally accepted.

* See, for example, in " Lives of the Poets," the final paragraph on
Addison's prose.

All this ease and comfort has now disappeared. The critic's task has become co-extensive with philosophy, history, psychology and all life itself. Though it be true that the task may be often shirked and running commentary of the most banal kind substituted for criticism, the critic who strives for truth has reason, and more than enough opportunity, to realise his own frail humanity. Yet his penitential exercises and humble confessions need not be unmitigated : he may comfort himself by rising from his solitary meditations and looking out of his window upon the mass of his fellow men. He cannot attain the perfect criticism, it is true : but, at least, in his activity he can come as near perfection as they in theirs, and the human virtues which they display can be his, since he cannot have the virtues of the angels. There are room for many virtues in criticism, and the critic who exercised them all would indeed make his critical activity a sublunary imitation of the perfect type. No two mental equipments are alike. This man may have a subtler penetration, that man a more orderly mind, but in his own way every critic may try to be accurate, not only in his main facts and deductions, but also in those little airy and unstable judgments by the way that come so glibly to the pen and by their very assurance most easily deceive the multitude ; he can try to be logical, since he must work by argument, to form his premises clearly and study his connections, to search his own thoughts for inconsistencies and not refuse, out of false pride or laziness, to reconcile them, and to avoid the temptation to dress out feeble judgments in the sham finery of an emotional appeal ; he can try to have insight, or to make what he has keener by practise and by study ; he can try to be sympathetic, even when his instinct prompts him to be cold or harsh, remembering that the perpetration of inferior art, though its inferiority may justly be exposed, is a misfortune rather than a crime. Such are the intellectual virtues of a critic : there are moral virtues too. Matthew Arnold rightly insisted that the critic should be disinterested, and few critical virtues have greater value, for the breath of vanity and the taint of spite are fatal infections ; even too strong a gust of ambition may nip a promising growth. But to be disinterested i not to be indifferent : he is a poor critic who cannot both love and loathe, rejoice and be angry, however calmly he may express himself. Any amount of devotion short of idolatry, any measure of love short of infatuation can be fruitfully spent by the critic. And the critic will try to be just, charitable and, above all, honest, for in the bustle of the literary market-place much false coin is uttered and passes from hand to hand ; and how easily it slips out on to the counter only a practising critic knows. Yet the critic himself must be wary, to avoid being deceived by new cries or old prejudices : he must always be sane himself and under control, but, like a doctor, understand the uncontrolled and the abnormal. He must have common sense in abundance, yet not too insistently demand it in the artist. And then, at the end, if he has successfully walked upon this difficult but honourable path, with small reward and less praise, it may be said of him what Professor Saintsbury, in his " History of English Criticism," said of Johnson : "We may freely disagree with his judgments, but we can never justly disable his judgment ; and this is the real criterion of a great critic."* A human critic could ask for no more favourable criticism.

Of virtue, then, the critic's glance out of his window will teach him to think rightly : but, more than that, it will enable him to

* *Op. cit.* p. 229.

estimate reasonably his relation to the rest
of humanity. Human criticism, even the most
inspired and the most judicious, is never out
of space and time : every critic belongs to his
generation, to his nation, to his family. He
has had the education of his period : he and
his contemporaries have reacted to the same
influences as they have breathed the same air.
The artists of one generation differ from those
of another in their outlook of life and in the
particular problems which they are impelled
to solve ; so do the critics : and the achievements of either, new and startling though they
may have been at their birth, may equally
survive to take on the venerable tone and the
restful serenity of old masters. But it must
be insisted once more that here, too, the perfection of human activity is rooted in imperfection,
in the imperfection of the time series. The
wise critic observing himself and his fellow-
practitioners, will not presume that he or they
can attain the undistorted view of eternity.
As he is not immune from the sorrows and the
catastrophies of his day, such as the recent
European war, so he cannot be impervious to
the conflicting winds of contemporary opinion
nor unaffected by changes in the direction of
contemporary interest. Though it may be

rash to speak of the " spirit of an age," as seeming to impose a false unity on what must at any moment be a bewildering variety, yet the variety of one age, which criticism attempts to reduce to order, differs from the variety of another.

There have been ages in our literature when violent invective, when vigorous satire, when an almost religious fervour, were the common accompaniments of criticism : they are not its accompaniments to-day. Another " Dunciad " would not be applauded, and a repetition of Matthew Arnold's first essay in criticism would seem to be often beside the mark. The critic, therefore, with all his ideal aspirations towards a more perfect state, need not be ashamed of belonging to his own generation, from which he cannot get away. And he will not attain perfection, either, by imagining that criticism is an exact science, expressed in symbols and equations that preserve the same efficacy for centuries. Words are his symbols, as they are the poet's ; and even words change their meaning. Nor need he waste his time in regretting the particular opportunities of his own age and longing for those of another. It is for him to please as well as to instruct, and he is not degraded by paying some attention to the demands of his audience. The perfect criticism, it is true, would involve the perfect medium and the perfect audience, yet all these are ideals, useful but remote. In practice he may perceive that Dryden's lines :

> Those who have best succeeded on the stage ,
> Have still conformed their genius to their age,

have an application, not to poetry alone, but also to criticism.

II

PRESENT CONDITIONS OF ENGLISH LITERARY CRITICISM

ENGLISH writers of our day seldom pause, I should say, to survey impartially the present conditions of literature. Critical journalists, it is true, at certain seasons of the year write hasty summaries of the year's poems, novels, pictures or music, but in these summaries a great deal is assumed without definition or analysis, for the writers of them usually rely upon the great British public's hazy consciousness of its own state of mind. Our writers would find it a useful exercise in clearing their own ideas if they were more frequently required to write comprehensive articles for a foreign public, provided that they had sufficient knowledge of that public—and very rarely would they have it—to understand what would need to be analysed and made clear. Many English critics, glib and assured enough in an English periodical, would find that there was many a knot to be disentangled

in their minds before they could answer clearly
and intelligibly an interested Frenchman or
Italian who should ask them, for instance,
what were the present tendencies and developments in English criticism ? The vast literary
market-place of English letters is not sharply
divided throughout into sections over which
Romanticists, Classicists, Impressionists and
Moralists jealously hang up their respective
banners. To an intelligent foreign observer
it might even seem that there were no dis-
tinctions at all—nothing but a confused
hurrying to and fro : a curious American
or an anxious watcher in one of the Empire's
Dominions might well find difficulty in des-
crying the dominant currents and personalities.
Indeed, it is not easy for those in the market-
place itself to formulate the results of their
own observations in terms that will give a
precise meaning to cultured men of another
country : it is a salutary effort, therefore.
What follows here, with all its imperfections,
is an effort of this kind.

One of our critics has remarked that England
has produced a prodigious number of men of
genius but comparatively few works of art :
but agreement with this pronouncement
depends upon the definition of a work of art.

It would be less disputable to say that England, though she has always bred great intellects, is not the home of a generically intellectual race. In other words, if there is such a thing as the English mind in general, it certainly does not lean towards analysis and criticism. We English are by nature practical, even in the domain of thought : as Sara Coleridge put it in a note to the " Biographia Literaria " : " The vice of the English mind in the present age, as many feel, is its pseudo-practicality ; everything treated of must issue in something to be *done* forthwith and outwardly, to be enjoyed sensuously or sentimentally." It is not a result of choice or of any particular time, but of heredity, rather, and possibly of environment ; and no single word sums up with absolute precision this quality of ours, in which both our virtues and our defects take part. It has often enough been made a subject of reproach to us by foreign critics, though—to speak of literature alone—our great figures, from Chaucer and Shakespeare onwards, have proved that we are not merely a nation of shopkeepers : but we are practical in the sense that we prefer to solve our problems by practice rather than by reflection. The old solution of a difficulty " ambulando," or by walking it off, has been typical of our methods. Moreover, Englishmen have always had an unreasonable mistrust for labels : and, though we have often been called a nation of eccentrics, we ourselves are inclined to call eccentric the man who devises and follows without compromise a logical theory.

This attitude of the English mind is, without doubt, an important condition, and to some extent a limitation, of criticism, as it is a factor in the main current of our literature : and the very fact that in Fnglish letters there is no sharp line of division between literature and criticism is a sign of it. Any one who reads such a book as Professor Saintsbury's " History of English Criticism " will see that most of our great critics have been poets and essayists rather than philosophers. Dryden, Johnson, Coleridge, Hazlitt, Macaulay, Matthew Arnold—to mention a few names— influenced the literature and taste of their time by commenting on the work of other writers rather than by examining the principles of artistic creation. In all our countless studies and monographs, even in our critical polemics and apologies, there are few parallels to Croce's " Estetica," nor is there often to be observed that attitude of purely analytical disinterestedness which seems to come naturally to the best French critics. We have had moments of pure philosophy—the moment of Locke, Berkeley and Hume, and the more modern moment of Mr. Bertrand Russell—but we have had no such moment in literary aesthetics. That is to say, we seldom find discussed at serious length the fundamental nature of the judgments upon which criticism rests. Professor Saintsbury quite frankly dismisses the inquiry as having nothing to do with criticism : and it would seem obvious, so far as public opinion goes, that a book like Dr. Bosanquet's on the philosophy of aesthetics has little influence compared with that of some sounding passage from the moralist Ruskin, or the impressionist Pater. The advantage of this mental trait—and one cannot doubt its disadvantages—is that the bulk of our best literary criticism is itself literature : it has style, colour and form, it includes many pages of the finest English prose, it is seldom pedantic or doctrinaire. The very fact that it is more ready to skim over the surface of literary art than to dig down to its roots gives it grace and movement. It has been the work of artists rather than of professors. So it remains to-day, pleasant to read but less easy to remember. The taste of our critics, perhaps, is more excellent than their principles. A friendly survey of English criticism to-day would provide a wealth of illustration for Professor Saintsbury's remark* on Dryden :

"He established (let us hope for all time) the English fashion of criticising, as Shakespeare did the English fashion of dramatising—the fashion of aiming at delight, at truth, at justice, at nature, at poetry, and letting the rules take care of themselves."

But to this must be appended the subsequent sign of the Professor's honesty, the words of qualification :

"It may be granted that Dryden did not escape the dangers of the process itself, the dangers of vagueness, of desultoriness, of dilettantism."

However, this anti-critical, anti-intellectual bias of the English mind is something more than a mere negation, or a source of agreeable embellishments to conceal mental vacuity. On its positive side it is powerful, almost portentous. On this side it appears as an

* In his "History of English Criticism," pp. 129-131

intense interest in morality, conduct, duty,
ethical religion, call it what you will, which,
since the Reformation, has been a vital factor
in the development of the English mind.
M. André Chevrillon, in his penetrating study
of Kipling's poetry (" Three Studies in English
Literature ") says that the practical and religious beliefs underlying Kipling's poetry are
" the common ground of all English culture " ;
and he says this only after exposing in a
masterly manner exactly what he means by
these beliefs and how they are illustrated
by the object of his study. Though objection
may fairly be made that M. Chevrillon
does not take into account the peculiar
deficiencies of the ethical attitude which
seems to inspire some of the robust "men
of action " poems in question, this does
not prevent the fourth section of his study,
headed " The Ethics of Kipling," from being
a forcible and truthful analysis which few
Englishmen could read without interest, assent
and admiration. This is not the place to sum-
marise or analyse it at length, but it is worth
while briefly to note that, to the mind of this
distinguished French critic, the English idea
of morality, duty or conduct is a " living,
dynamic idea, inspiring enthusiasm ;   a

vehemence of divine essence and origin,
partaking of the driving force of the world."
He remarks that it is found sufficient in our
churches when dogma tends to disappear,
and he continues :

"Hence the lyrical intensity which often
surprises us in the preaching of Carlyle and
Ruskin, as in the more ethical poems of Wordsworth and Tennyson—those, in fact, which
the English public has always loved. For
this public responds to such accents ; more
than any other it is sensitive to an order of
beauty that appeals only to the soul ; and this
we recognise when we reproach our neighbours
for looking upon art as a vehicle for moral
ideas. More than any other is this public
capable of grave enthusiasm for spiritual
grandeur . . . ."

These words are quoted in no spirit of complacency here, for any decent English conscience
should be perfectly aware of all that is to be
said on the other side : but they are quoted
as opportune in the very discussion in which
we are engaged, and another sentence of
M. Chevrillon's makes it clear in what manner.
He says : "Now that the critical spirit has

at last made its way into England, Kipling, of all the great living writers of his country, stands alone for the absolute in ethics, with a militant faith. A Wells, a Shaw, a Bennett, a Galsworthy, serve other gods, the gods of reason or of sentiment." There is a good deal in this judgment which is surprising and which, on another occasion, would be worth a searching examination : but the point here is that the English idea of conduct, vital and profound as it is, strikes the French critic as being the antithesis of the critical spirit. It is true, of course, that the critical spirit to which he is here particularly referring, is that which inquires into the constitution of society and the relations of its members ; but the observation holds good generally. Indeed, it would be strange if a creative literature so strongly inspired as ours is by this idea should have found a purely intellectual criticism to interpret t. We know that it has not, nor does it now : and though it may be true to say that the critical spirit has at last made its way to England, it is not easy to say where it is to be found unadulterated. Indeed, if—contrary to M. Chevrillon—one holds that in the work of Wells, Shaw, Arnold Bennett and Galsworthy this old idea is rampant, it may be that even in the most aesthetically minded of our literary critics it is rampant also. And if it be asked where, in contemporary criticism, the idea itself is to be found most unblushingly present, the critical work of the late Mr. Clutton Brock, of Mr. John Bailey and of Mr. Middleton Murry may be indicated, on the higher level, and the review columns of all the English daily and weekly papers, on the lower.

Even so, we cannot yet dismiss the English temperament, as an element in English criticism. Its practical, or moral, bias, which in creative literature leads us to emphasise and enjoy action rather than reflection, the delineation of character rather than the analysis of motive, and the intensity of emotion rather than intensity of expression, cannot but have a directive, though occasionally antagonistic, influence upon criticism ; and this is illustrated every day in the common tendency of English critics to consider works of art primarily as manifestations of their creators' individual characters. But there is another typical, though not universal, quality of the English temperament which is also not without its effect upon the arts and criticism of them.

This is the tendency to mysticism which, like a strange, fiery and eruptive stratum, lies deep beneath the bony rock of our northern natures, and has issued, through the ages, in many forms, now in clear fire, now in vague but impressive mist, but freely accompanied all the time, so far as men and women at large were concerned, by sheer lumps of stupidity. Mysticism, as a process, has no more value in itself than other processes of knowledge : it is the results which are to be estimated, and the results of bad and imperfect mysticism are assuredly vanity. But to disregard its influence, to deny its triumphs, to make no attempt to understand it, is to turn one's back on some of the greatest achievements of literature and to misjudge others which are less than great. No age of our literature was without it, and many were pervaded by it : to catalogue our poetry alone under that heading would be a long and unnecessary proceeding. Shakespeare alone would take up many pages. The evidence of it in our prose is equally overwhelming. The point need not be laboured. But it is worth observing that with this tendency to mysticism another traditional British quality, independence, is closely connected. In a controversial article in *The Adelphi** Mr. Middleton Murry discussed this fact with some spirit. Without entering for the moment into the merits of the particular discussion, which centred on the question whether or no Classicism existed in English literature, I quote some of his words as an illustration of my own remarks. He said :

" The English writer, the English divine, the English statesman, inherit no rules from their forbears : they inherit only this : a sense that in the last resort they must depend upon the inner voice. If they dig deep enough in their pursuit of self-knowledge—a piece of mining done not with the intellect alone, but with the whole man—they will come upon a self that is universal : in religious terms, the English tradition is that the man who truly interrogates himself will ultimately hear the voice of God, in terms of literary criticism that the writer achieves impersonality through personality."

And again, in the same article :

" Catholicism stands for the principle of unquestioned spiritual authority outside the

* For September, 1923.

individual; that is also the principle of classicism in literature. The English nature is instinctively rebellious to such a principle."

There could be no more direct and forcible statement of the mystical, independent spirit which is typical of the English temperament. It is to be found all over the pages of Meredith and Carlyle, and, perhaps, its most grandiose expression in modern prose is to be found in Herman Melville's "Moby Dick," which is a great work of English literature though not written by an Englishman. Further, to add the testimony of one who affected to deplore it, but in secret was too representative an Englishman not to sympathise with it, I may quote the opinion of Dr. Johnson :*

" In absolute governments there is sometimes a general reverence paid to all that has the sanction of power, and the countenance of greatness. How little this is the state of our country needs not to be told. We live in an age in which it is a kind of public sport to refuse all that cannot be enforced. The edicts of an English Academy would probably be read by many, only that they might be sure

* Lives of the Poets. *Roscommon.*

to disobey them. That our language is in
perpetual danger of corruption cannot be
denied ; but what prevention can be found ?
The present manners of the nation would
deride authority and therefore nothing is left
but that every writer should criticise himself."

Dr. Johnson, of course, was here thinking
of a particular question, the possibility of
preserving our tongue by the edicts of an
academy : but what he says is generally true,
in England, of all edicts in all ages. So far,
then, as criticism can be taken to represent an
outward authority and to embody an imposed
tradition, this quality in the English temperament is opposed to it, as it was opposed, in
politics, to the extremes of the Tory creed ;
though this creed, in its turn, is also deeply
rooted in the English temperament. It is
not uninteresting, therefore, to find Mr. T. S.
Eliot and his friends who stand bold and
outright for Classicism, speaking of the
tendencies that oppose their preaching of a
literary " Church and State " as " Whiggery "
tendencies. The opposition goes down to the
foundations of criticism and needs a chapter
to itself : but its existence is evidence that the
tendencies of the English temperament itself

are important conditions of criticism. To an observer one thing is clear, namely, that the "Whiggery" tendencies have numbers, though by no means all the discrimination and sensibility, on their side : for it is obvious that, while a supreme interest in practice or morals, a preference for the inner voice over extant tradition and a recalcitrant attitude to a not freely chosen authority, may be articulated into clear and comprehensive principles, they also lend themselves to adoption by the unintelligent and the lazy-minded, on whom a severe course of literary Toryism would have a regenerative effect. The fact is that the critics of genuine understanding are an infinitesimal minority of the English public which reads. This is another condition of criticism which must be taken into account.

No foreigner, certainly, could frame a clear idea of English literary taste without some knowledge of the general state of literary culture in England, or unless he were endowed with the special gift of insight which made M. Abel Chevalley's book " Le Roman Anglais de notre Temps " so remarkable a piece of criticism. One would have to take him by the hand to study carefully the overflowing counters of a bookstall in one of our large railway stations, and then to let him stand and listen for an afternoon to the conversation that passed in a general bookshop between the customers and the shop assistants. After some experience in a public library, a suburban and a university literary society, and a month's hard reading of British periodicals, he would begin to have a glimmering notion of what contemporary literary taste might mean if the expression were to cover the whole of the observed facts. Our reading public is vast, and stretches down from the most highly and truly educated far away below the line of those who can afford to be well educated, if they wish. It is as difficult to say where it ends as where it begins. Many levels of taste are to be observed in it, and these do not correspond to the different levels of the nicely distinguished social classes. Those who live upon the highest levels are here, as everywhere, few : but these few are not—as they may more often be in countries where the general public is less well educated—dictators of literary taste and fashion. On the contrary, so huge is the number of those whose reading is on the level of the merely entertaining or sensational, that these loftier spirits cannot easily make their voices heard. Also, there is a remarkable force in the movement for self-education. Institutions for teaching all kinds of subjects, from poetry to photography, by correspondence have a host of clients ; and there seems to be in the breasts of the young and eager a feverish desire to increase their knowledge—and their market value—by quick and not too difficult methods. This ardent class of students is liberally provided for by the press. Side by side with the more intellectual weekly journals, such as " The Spectator " and " The Nation," exists the type of " John o' London's Weekly," which only costs threepence and brings news of letters to thousands in a popular form. Cheap editions, not only of the classics, but of all types of literature, are produced by many of the publishing houses. Thus, the " Everyman Library " of Messrs. Dent, Bell's " Popular Classics " and the " Home University Library," published by Messrs. Williams and Norgate provide handy introductions to all branches of thought and to the study of the chief European literatures.

It is true that this multitude of energetic but not very highly educated readers, to say nothing of those who daily drug themselves with what is simply bad literature, is not directly reached, as a rule, by the newest developments of thought and criticism ; but they have their effect, nevertheless, upon literary production. Their custom is so profitable that no publisher can safely neglect it, and they are a rich potential public for any writer who can touch their imagination. This very fact makes publishers chary of investing their money in works which are only likely to have a limited circulation, and since this is always the fate of serious criticism, criticism suffers accordingly. It is significant that Mr. Well's " Universal History " a work of genius in spite of its faults, was produced with this class mainly in view, in fortnightly parts each costing one and threepence. Less valuable compilations in the same form have imitated it, and the day may come when a series entitled " Criticism through the Ages," with pictures of Aristotle and of Sainte-Beuve's home, may bring the critic once more into the popular eye. Any work or any theory which is to have a wide circulation, at all events, must touch the higher fringe of these readers, especially as their taste is chiefly appealed to by almost the whole of the daily press. In this respect conditions in England are very different from those of a hundred and more years ago. In the day of

Byron, Keats and Shelley a critical article in the " Quarterly " or the " Edinburgh " was a matter of high importance in the world of letters. But nowadays the opinions expressed in the quarterly reviews have no reverberations in public opinion at large, and the verdicts of individual critics, in general, exercise small influence upon the majority of men and women who read.

One result of these conditions in England— it might be truer, perhaps, to say one accompaniment—is a general sanity, if anything but a delicacy, of taste. The extravagant perversions of art, the morbid psychology, the extreme applications of new aesthetic theory, which show themselves from time to time on the continent of Europe, find little echo in England but that of mild laughter. Signor Marinetti, when he visited us, was only a joke; and attempts to introduce musical and literary degeneracies from France lately have had no success. Except in certain small cliques the accepted literary art is, at least, reasonable; and even the highly developed minds in England are not, as a rule, partisans of particular and exclusive theories. A glance at our literary periodicals is enough to show this : so far as letters are concerned, there is hardly anything to distinguish them but their titles and their shapes. The quarterlies and the monthlies, in general, have no hard and fast literary programmes, nor could it be predicated of any particular contribution in which of them it must infallibly have appeared. The reviewers of new books differ from one another in their idiosyncrasies and methods of approach, but the review columns to which they contribute have an almost irritating likeness. There is, undoubtedly, a value in this impartiality, which is to be remarked, in particular, in the " Literary Supplement " of " The Times," which covers the whole field of English, besides a good deal of foreign literature, and draws its reviewers, all of whom write anonymously, from the men of letters, historians, scientists, and the learned men in general of the whole country. This remarkable periodical—the envy of European countries where reviewing is neither disinterested nor uninfluenced by political animosity—is one in which our literary world takes a legitimate pride and a weekly pleasure, though nobody regards any of its judgments as necessarily infallible. On the whole, it represents the best of English criticism : it is typical rather than individual—the co-operative work of a large number of workers, connected by no tie even of personal acquaintance, save by chance, and directed by one who, in criticism, is an admirable critic only of his own contributors. And this uniformity in diversity, of which the "Literary Supplement" is so striking an example, is made easy by the English preference in criticism for appreciation over analysis. An average English reader of reviews and literary studies desires general enlightenment on the nature and value of the work discussed rather than a dissection of its vital structure from which its value would be left to be inferred. But the danger of this safe but somewhat indolent state of mind is that it encourages laxity of taste and want of discrimination : and its result is that, besides the work of genuine critics, there are many ill-written books published, and devoured by a very imperfectly educated public, which are composed on the principle of ecstatically praising the work of all authors in whom there is the slightest enjoyment to be found. The writers of these books corrupt the literary palate of their generation by encouraging their readers to gorge themselves promiscuously. The mental indigestion which results from this diet is a common malady in England,

The above description of the English reading public is summary and incomplete, but my aim was to display it as a contemporary condition to which criticism is obliged to adapt itself. The paramount influence of a small and cultivated body of people, which creates the most favourable atmosphere for authoritative and profound criticism, is no longer a possibility : if there be a court of letters, it has small authority and earns little respect even among the courtiers. Moreover, the irresistible pressure forwards of new hordes of readers, with small means and less leisure, with boundless desires for entertainment but with brains too tired with daily labour or too cramped by environment for serious reflection, has created a kind of revolt against a standard of artistic taste, which is, or may seem to be, at all subtle or fastidious. The likes and dislikes of the " plain man " are trumpeted abroad with contemptuous flourishes, as if they would be constant and decisive test of merit till the Day of Judgment. Good, honest cabbages, it is proclaimed, are better plants than your sensitive orchids or your carefully grown roses : art must come out of the hothouse and be freed from the manure heap. These protests are not wholly ill-founded : priggishness and

coterie-cult deserve all the opprobrium that
may be their lot, but that the protesters may
go a little far can be illustrated from an article
published not long ago in " The London
Mercury "* by Mr. J. C. Stobart on "Modern
Taste." In the course of this article, which was
written in a style of humorous petulance not
to be taken too seriously, he wrote :

" The truth is that the last few generations
have developed a rich man's culture which
is to some extent out of touch with the appetite
of the mass of our town-dwelling countrymen
. . . . A deal of the work that critics praise
in all the arts was done to win the praise of
critics. Everything that is subtle, learned,
allusive, satirical, ironic, introspective, exotic
was wrought by or for people well-nourished,
or perhaps a trifle over-fed, in the intellectual
sense. The novels of Meredith, for example,
were written for idle folk about idle folk.
Scarcely any of his people have a definite
occupation in life, if we except a schoolmaster,
a tutor, a journalist and a diplomat or two
who enjoy, of course, very long vacations.
Most of the literature written in England during
the last fifty years presupposes a well-to-do

* For January, 1924.

reader who will be familiar through travel with foreign countries, have acquaintance with precedence and etiquette, and who will have had leisure during innumerable holidays to study nature, climb mountains and infest picture galleries and libraries. Most of the modern lyrical poetry with its extreme devotion to nightingales, lesser celandines, bathers, white owls, old ruins, rural landscapes, romantic young females, elaborate psychological experiences and so forth was written for comfortable people who enjoy protracted holidays in the country and like to sit by the fire in Grosvenor Square during the winter and read about these things. Fortunately, it is only a part of poetry, a fraction of literature, a fragment of the great body of English culture."

The last remark is true, but it is hardly necessary to point out in detail the falsities and half-truths of the rest. Even the last remark condemns by implication Shakespeare's sonnets, as an earlier generalisation practically accuses Wordsworth, Keats and Shelley of writing for the enjoyment of Grosvenor Square. And since when did Grosvenor Square support the finer shades in literature ? A very good case, on the contrary, might be made out for the view that in literature, as in society at large, to use the words of a lugubrious ditty, " It's only the poor that help the poor." I am afraid that nearly all our lyric poets receive scanty sustenance from Mayfair, but Mr. Stobart thinks otherwise. At any rate, he roundly says :

"Art has this tendency to specialise away from life and become a mystery. It is a professional failing to adopt a jargon, a ritual, and to exclude strangers. Critics ought to fight the tendency. Critics ought to hold a brief for plain people, because when art becomes etiolated it grows sick."

And it was because certain critics held these views a hundred years ago that they abused Wordsworth, Keats and Shelley whose poems, or some of them, having become familiar, are now found comforting and inspiring by a vast number of plain people. All great things are a mystery, whether you call them art or life, and it is futile to write as if people for whom it is too much trouble to think had the monopoly of wholesome truth : and if, in the present day, some art and some criticism have become alembicated it is, in part, in

revolt against the triviality and vulgarity that
spread themselves so insistently over beauty
and fineness. It is one thing to abandon
criticism altogether as being on a low level
compared with action and contemplation,
and quite another to suggest that criticism
should give up its freedom and its tools, abandon
its search for the essential amid the transitory,
and adopt the attitude of a keeper of tame but
hungry animals who should cry aloud : " It is
forbidden to feed these animals with cooked
food." Besides, there is no necessity : there
are already the publishers.

I have endeavoured to describe the environment of criticism in this country, the soil
from which, being English, it must grow, and
the atmosphere, also English, in which it must
put forth its leaves. It is hardly to be wondered
at if a foreign observer should find it rather a
bushy growth, with shallow roots and a
somewhat rank florescence, ornamental in the
mass but rarely suited for exhibition. It is
not surprising if the critical biography or
monograph, a literary genre in which we excel,
and in which the delineation of an author's
worldly figure, gracefully and sympathetically
carried out, is agreeably illustrated by allusion
to his works, prevails over the really determined

focusing of thought upon the work of art alone ; nor that in most of our periodicals where books and writers are discussed entertaining commentary and graceful appreciation, with all urbanity of style, should be found in profusion, but that grasp of historical connection, interest in sequence of ideas and fierce desire to capture artistic truth for its own sake are seldom to be found. Want of individual aptitude and of public interest account for the fact that enormous arrears of critical work remain to be done if our criticism is to be worthy of our literature. Only a few languid spades have been lifted in the pressing task of thoroughly excavating the great literary field of the mid-nineteenth century : a few odd bones have been happily brought to light amid general congratulations, but the real business of thoroughly clearing away the detritus of prejudice, ignorance and sentiment which hides the skeleton of this age has hardly been begun. For the same reason, we are bare of conclusions about the literature of the immediate past and the actual present. On the poets and creative writers from Swinburne onwards contemporary judgment is partial and fluctuating. Veneration and horror still equally attend the work of Mr. Thomas Hardy and Mr. Rudyard Kipling : irrelevances enwrap that of Mr. Bernard Shaw, Mr. Wells, Mr. Galsworthy, Mr. D. H. Lawrence, and modern poetry is still a battlefield. The labour of tidying-up, were it seriously undertaken, would be colossal, and there is no inducement to undertake it. We seem to look in vain for an intellect large enough, a knowledge wide enough, and a disinterested energy powerful enough to force order upon this confusion. Even the most enlightened critical judgments may be superseded in the progress of time, but the order produced by truly penetrating and authoritative criticism remains for ever. The statement of this unfortunate fact is no moral reflection upon critics who do not feel drawn to this self-sacrifice, still less a denial of their individual excellences in their less exalted activities. It would be almost a miracle if such an intellect were to arise and devote itself to the task under present conditions : but to deny the need of it would be blindness. And, since one day or another, with Time's inexorable tidiness, order will come, it is to be hoped that we shall not suffer the humiliation of seeing our own neglected task accomplished by a foreign critic.

III

THE IMPULSES TO CRITICISM

In examining so loosely connected a whole as
the body of contemporary criticism some
guiding principle is necessary for the clear
grouping of individual performances. The
construction and investigation of a mere
nominal catalogue is always an arid process,
and the importance of its result is usually
disproportionate to the burden which it lays
upon the powers of assimilation. As an
improvement on mere enumeration other
principles suggest themselves. There is the
point of view, for instance, of aesthetic
philosophy, from which the critics' approxima-
tions to a complete theory of art in literature
might be analysed and compared ; there is the
point of view of pure literature, from which
the various critical works might be criticised
as art and be judged by their approach to an
ideal of standard literary excellence ; there
are, again, divisions in the subject matter
of criticism—ancient literature, modern

literature, poetry, drama, fiction, and so forth
—in applying their minds to which different
critics might be shown to have different
excellences ; and there some wandering terms,
ready like strolling players to assume many
disguises, to be found on the roads of literature
—terms such as Classic, Romantic, Realist,
Impressionist—which we might rig out as
rival captains, pick up sides for them, and
count the points in the ensuing tournament.
There are imperfections, however, in all these
points of view. To the first the objection
is that the development of an aesthetic
philosophy is not the aim of criticism, but is
presupposed in a critic, even if it has not been
logically articulated by him ; to the second
the objection is that the degree of literary
beauty attained by a critic's work is not an
essential criterion by which to judge criticism,
the virtues of which are insight, adequacy
and truth ; and to the third, the division of
criticism by subject matter, though it might
lead to conclusions of a certain transitory
interest, the objection is that it would be an
arbitrary division, with the defects, and without
the exhaustiveness, of a nominal catalogue.
For the dressing up of rival captains from
among the wandering " tendencies " something

more might be said ; but the difficulty would be to keep these captains from changing their appearances, and even their sides, before the match was over. There was promise in a division once drawn by Mr. T. S. Eliot between the historical, philosophical and poetic critics ; but he had no sooner drawn it than he withdrew the name of critic from the first two kinds : and Mr. Middleton Murry, after being at some pains in one book* to combat this division by proving that the only worthy critic was the philosophic, in a later book† took more kindly to it, remarking that, as a work of literature might have historical, ethical or aesthetic significance, so a critic is bound to have a predisposition to one of these kinds of significance, while a perfect critic would combine them all in equal parts. This uncertainty on the part of two authorities warns us of imperfections in any division of critics by their dispositions to the significances. It will be better to look elsewhere.

There is, I think, a simpler and more fundamental principle of division, which is free from the objection that the relating of individuals to significances outside themselves, without

* " Aspects of Literature," *The Function of Criticism.*
† " Countries of the Mind," *A Critical Credo.*

their express permission, is a little dangerous and presumptuous, like deducing a man's politics from the newspapers which he is observed to read. Mr. Middleton Murry speaks of " predispositions," and he is right. All human beings have particular predispositions, and it is clear that only a perfect— and therefore ideal, non-human—being could combine conflicting, if complementary, predispositions in equal parts. If, then, there is any substance in the views put forward in the preceding chapters ; if the conception of perfect criticism is only valuable as an unattainable ideal, and if human criticism is affected by the external influences of its time and conditioned by the qualities of the minds which produce and demand it, a good working principle of division for the present purpose may, perhaps, be found in men's predispositions, not to kinds of significance, but to something more intimate and individual. Significances are well enough as terms of convenience, but they are generic terms and, therefore, abstractions. Activities, on the contrary, are neither generic nor abstract, for we are intimately conscious of our activities at all moments of our waking life : they are our private possessions, and to some extent unique and incomparable. Yet their uniqueness is more one of colouring than of essence, so that in comparing and relating them under common names the abstraction is a small one. The activity of laughter in one man, for instance, or his predisposition to it, is strictly comparable to that of another : also, if a man be seen laughing, there is no presumption in speaking of his disposition to laughter. And so, with critics, we shall be on surer ground if we try to find a principle of grouping in their observed activities, for these will reveal to us their predispositions or, to look at them from another angle, their primary impulses to criticism.

Criticism is not a mere negation : sheer fault-finding, slandering and abuse would not be criticism at all. Criticism has always a positive aim : it is a creation, or at least a presentation, of something real, felt by an individual, even though it appear as the thinnest shadow of an idea barely discernible through heavy veils of irrelevance and vapours of prejudice. It is an intellectual expression in literary form of a positive mental activity, and the activities expressed will vary with the predispositions of individuals. I suggest, without claiming that it is a complete or exhaustive classification, that three main types of activity are discernible in criticism. There is, first, the activity of creation itself, similar in kind though not in intensity, to that which brings forth art and poetry : there is, second, the patient but passionate activity of inquiry, which animates the disinterested investigations of pure science ; and there is, also, the simply practical activity, which is that of attaining a preconceived useful end by appropriate means and effort—the activity which finds its outlet primarily in *doing* something to satisfy a rational and practical impulse, a vast activity of bound-less energy and infinite adaptability to every variety of human task, from darning socks to building bridges. In criticism the task is that of pronouncing a particular judgment upon a particular case, of advising, of refining contemporary taste, of fulfilling a demand made by the public and, no less than in artistic creation, of pleasing an audience. But the emphasis of the activity is mainly upon the performance itself, and its performances are judged, not so much by their ultimate signifi-cance or their absolute truth, as by their adequacy and usefulness. These three activities are not completely contradictory or mutually exclusive : they are, ideally, complementary, though, practically, often in conflict. Since they are real, easily recognisable and extensive, they will be here adopted as convenient divisions under which to range types of criticism. The true principle of variation is the predisposition of the critic, which is an unavoidable and not always perfectly conscious fact, howsoever highly it may be rationalised ; and every critic is likely to reveal in the course of his writings to which activity he is chiefly predisposed.

To those who study criticism at all these three types are familiar in common observation. The primarily creative type of critic is usually the richest, the most intense in expression, and at moments may reach to a momentary fusion of thought and vision which are analogous to the inevitable and eternal moments of great poetry. On the other hand, it is not the clearest and most consistent over its whole course, for no steady wind controls it, but gusts of emotion perturb it and irritations of defeated creative instinct, like submarine currents, deflect it from its purpose. And all the deceptions which attend the work of imagination are its dangers : self-delusion, empty vagueness, mere sensationalism shadowy transcendentalism, hollow rhetoric—

these are some of its besetting faults. At its best, in the sudden incandescence of a great spirit, it will throw off a brightness that, like a new star from a nebula, takes its place for ever in the firmament of literature : but its brightness may also be as brief and transitory as a show of fireworks, and, at its worst, it may degenerate into the crackling of rubbish on a bonfire. It may be a matter of surprise that creative minds, whose natural impulse is to the expression of something deeply individual—whether this be called intuition, perception or emotion—should engage themselves in criticism, which is not a completely autonomous activity. Yet we know that they do so, either from want of creative energy, or lassitude, or curiosity, or anger, or a natural tendency to philosophic reflection. Poets have written criticism to illustrate or defend their poetry, philosophers that they might stamp their view of reality also upon letters, and moralists that they might assert a moral dominion over elusive art.

All the many types of creative mind, in fact, can be found reflected in criticism, giving ample illustration both of its felicities and its dangers. Critics of the inquiring activity are apt to regard their intrusion with mistrust. Mr. T. S. Eliot, for instance, in his essay on Hamlet in " The Sacred Wood," is not afraid to write :

" Hamlet the character has had an especial temptation for that most dangerous type of critic : the critic with a mind which is naturally of the creative order, but which through some weakness in creative power, exercises itself in criticism instead. These minds often find in Hamlet a vicarious existence for their own artistic realisation. Such a mind had Goethe, who made of Hamlet a Werther ; and such had Coleridge, who made of Hamlet a Coleridge ; and probably neither of these men in writing about Hamlet remembered that his first business was to study a work of art."

In his introduction to the same book, Mr. Eliot observes that in modern times, not only are the natural critics, the born questioners and correctors, tempted to abandon the criticism of art till they have cleaned up society, but that " criticism proper betrays such poverty of ideas and such atrophy of sensibility that men who ought to preserve their critical ability for the improvement of their own creative work are tempted into criticism."

These words contain much truth, but they are only quoted here as a testimony to the nature of the creative mind's impulse to criticism. However, it may not be only of their own emotions or their own irritations that the creative critics wish to be assertive : their sign, indeed, is that they wish passionately to confess or assert something personal, but it may be no more than a particular aesthetic sensibility, a particular religion or a particular view of morality in its relation to art. John Addington Symonds, Walter Pater and Ruskin, in their different ways, came within this category ; and in our own day, not only the impact of innumerable painful questions which assail us, but a passionate desire for an ideal reconstruction of shattered society, have helped the predispositions of younger men, such as Mr. Hugh Fausset and Mr. Middleton Murry, to find in criticism a medium for fervent moral homily. Art, Mr. Murry insists,* is the revelation of an ideal in human life ; and that ideal is a moral one, the ideal of the good life, and every act of art is a voluntary submission to this principle of its own sovereignty.

"True criticism is itself an organic part

* See notes to p. 67.

74

of the whole activity of art ; it is the exercise of sovereignty by art upon itself, and not the imposition of an alien. To use our previous metaphor, as art is the consciousness of life, criticism is the consciousness of art. The essential activity of true criticism is the harmonious control of art by art."

And again :

" Thus art reveals to us the principle of its own governance. The function of criticism is to apply it. Obviously it can be applied only by him who has achieved, if not the actual aesthetic ideal in life, at least a vision and a sense of it. He alone will know that the principle he has to elucidate and apply is living, organic. It is, indeed, the very principle of artistic creation itself."

Here blow transcendental breezes in which we easily recognise the type of Mr. Murry's critical activity. They blow still more strongly in Mr. Hugh Fausset's " Studies in Idealism," where in the preface he says :

" One of the functions of criticism should be, then, to help men to sublimate their emotions, to differentiate in poetry between the expression of the accidental sensation or personal

75

appetite and that which is rendered real and absolute by its rational content, so that we can say of it that it has the permanence of truth as well as the allurement of beauty. For the truest poetry is an experience of life realised in imagery and, partially, at least, disintegrated into thought, as distinct from a slavish imitation of life or a chain of thoughts suffused by feeling. An essential emotion can then be distinguished from an accidental, not only by the extent to which it moves us, but by the vital vision, the innate philosophy, which its expression disintegrates, and which is susceptible of analysis. True poetry embodies a profound apprehension of life : it relates particular experience to a body of past experience, subconsciously criticised, to the rhythm of universal nature, to the morality of human reason, so that the experiences of such a poet, though particular, are never trivial. For they are one with the life-principle, with that primary creative emotion in which all thought is contained."

This is, in fact, the completely transcendental view of poetry, full of vague terms which are indefinable, and susceptible of infinite grades of emotional colouring : the " life-principle " is typical, and so is the idea that all thought is contained in a primary creative emotion. However, I only quote here these statements from contemporary criticism as examples of the predisposition in criticism to creation or—what is only another aspect of it—to self-expression. The important thing to these minds is the attitude, the ultimate ideal, the philosophy. They are thirsty for the water brooks of ideal perfection, and they become wrathful at earthly denials of them. Yet they are not all transcendental. Even so logical a critic as Professor Croce is not wholly without this predisposition : it shows itself in his anxious elaboration of a complete philosophy to support his view of art, and flashes out like a sword in those vigorous paragraphs in which with trenchant words he decapitated contemptuously the paladins of all renegade and misdirected criticism. It is a natural attitude in minds of more than ordinary power and of strong moral purpose. We may, indeed we should, criticise such errors as it breeds in particular instances, but it is foolish to deny or belittle the fruits of it, when they are good, through any preconceived notions. Creative critics may often be inconsistent and unintelligible : they may often

77

speak beside the point : but they may speak also, as Coleridge did, with such exquisite truth that their fragmentary utterances outweigh whole centos of grave, serious and useful inquiry.

It is not necessary that criticism of·this type should be romantic : an earnest insistence upon a purely logical view of reality, such as Croce's, or a fierce but narrow Puritanism, such as that of the American critic Paul Elmer More, can find expression in it. Yet, since it is the most intimately and deeply personal type of criticism, it appears above all as a function of northern minds and romantic tendencies : and it is needless to say that the trend to individualistic mysticism which distinguishes the English mind on its speculative side indulges itself freely in criticism of this kind. In a note to a passage in one of his lectures on " The Problem of Style " Mr. Middleton Murry states this without reserve :

" But the pregnant distinction is not between the Romantic and the Realist, but between the Romantic and the Classical writer. This distinction is of the utmost importance, but it is rather philosophical and ethical than literary. The Classical writer feels himself to be a

member of an organised society, a man with
duties and restrictions imposed upon him
by a moral law which he deeply acknowledges.
The Romantic is in rebellion against external
law, and just as deeply refuses to acknowledge
its sanction. He asserts the rights of his
individuality *contra mundum* . . . . The point
to be remembered is that the judgment whether
a writer is Romantic or Classical is a moral
judgment, undoubtedly necessary to fundamental criticism, but out of place in the discussion of style."

From the day of Lamb and Coleridge to the
present this spirit has blown through English
criticism. In fact, its absence is more remarkable than its presence in some degree, even
when the dominating disposition is the purely
practical. It is absurd to regard it as a mere
delusion or a fantastic error, though it seem
frequently to lose its direction and arrive at
conclusions remote from its critical intention ;
for, like Don Quixote, it is often nobler in its
errors than respectable realists are in their
more orderly progressions. It is better, at all
events, to recognise with Professor Santayana,
a philosophical critic but no romantic, the
virtues inherent in this disposition. I quote

79

from his fine summing up of the matter at the conclusion of his lecture on Goethe's *Faust* ("Three Philosophical Poets"):

"In fact, the great merit of the romantic attitude in poetry, and of the transcendental method in philosophy, is that they put us back at the beginning of our experience. They disintegrate convention, which is often cumbrous and confused, and restore us to ourselves, to immediate perception and primordial will. That, as it would seem, is the true and inevitable starting point. Had we not been born, had we not peeped into this world, each out of his personal eggshell, the world might indeed have existed without us, as a thousand undiscoverable worlds may now exist; but for us it would not have existed. This obvious truth would not need to be insisted on but for two reasons: one that conventional knowledge, such as our notions of science and morality afford, is often top-heavy: asserts and imposes on us much more than our experience warrants—our experience which is our only approach to reality. The other reason is the reverse or counterpart of this; for conventional knowledge often ignores and seems to suppress parts of experience no less actual and important for us than those parts on which the conventional knowledge itself is reared. The public world is too narrow for the soul as well as too mythical and fabulous . . . . This Philosophy, as Kant said, is cathartic : it is purgative and liberating ; it is intended to make us start afresh and start right.

It follows that one who has no sympathy with such a philosophy is a comparatively conventional person. He has a second-hand mind . . . . It follows, also, however, that one who has no philosophy but this has no wisdom ; he can say nothing that is worth carrying away ; everything in him is attitude and nothing is achievement . . . .

To be miscellaneous, to be indefinite, to be unfinished, is essential to the romantic life. May we not say that it is essential to all life, in its immediacy ; and that only in reference to what is not life—to objects, ideals and unanimities that cannot be experienced but may only be conceived—can life become rational and truly progressive ? Herein we may see the radical and inalienable excellence of romanticism ; its sincerity, freedom, richness and infinity. Herein too, we may see its limitations, in that it cannot fix or trust any of its ideals, and blindly believes the universe to be as wayward as itself, so that nature and art are always slipping through its fingers. It is obstinately empirical, and will never learn anything from experience."

It is other people's experience, let it be observed, from which the romantics, critics or not, will not learn ; and their misfortune is that they can seldom translate into adequate and stable words that particular experience which they assert, with passion, to be sacred and their own.

The second type of activity to which critical predispositions may be observed is that of inquiry. It is one extension of the scientific analytic spirit which, exercised in its appropriate spheres, has exhibited triumphantly the possibilities of the human intellect. It would be superfluous to insist upon the noble fruits borne in mathematics, astronomy, physics and chemistry by man's primeval curiosity when controlled by intelligence and directed by imagination. It is a persistent but unemotional activity, turned outwards from itself. Self-expression has for it no interest and little meaning, for the self seems to it unimportant in comparison with the immensity and complexity of the external things to be observed. Truth and order are its aims, precision is its virtue. It is content to accept provisionally what has been handed down to it, since it has no desire to create experience for itself ; moreover, it soon learns to identify individuality more readily with error than with truth, with anarchy than with law. It wears, often, the appearance of coldness and remoteness from life, but a flame burns brightly at its inmost core, and its achievements, instead of passing away into the limbo of outworn ideas, become knit with the texture of knowledge. When it denies the efficacy of romanticism, being inevitably realist, romanticism sometimes retorts by objecting that its ideal is fundamentally a moral one, since, they say, truth cannot be sought until it be decided that it is good to know the truth. But this is really a false objection, for " good " in this judgment is empty of all moral content, from which it is ridiculous to proceed to the triumphant assertion that, even for the realist, the only ideal is the ideal of a good life. Pounding the pulpit will never persuade the purely scientific spirit that this is true, for he knows that it is not. The ideal before him, which he calls truth without necessarily

defining it, is something ultimate and unchange-
able, to which the ideal relation—and the
only possible one—is that of knowing, of pure
contemplation, not of living or feeling or
doing. As an ideal it is not self-contradictory
and it is humanly conceivable : not much more
can be said for any ideal present to a human
mind. Since any inquiry may be animated
by this spirit, and criticism cannot be conducted
without some inquiry, it may, and does,
animate criticism.

At this point, with all apologies to those
who are only interested in the strictly contemporary, it becomes necessary to speak of
Aristotle, who died more than two thousand
years ago but whose work is still full of life.
Aristotle was undoubtedly one of the most
remarkable incarnations of the purely inquiring
activity, though possibly, because we know so
little of his life, we imagine his scientific
spirit to be purer than it actually was. He
turned his mind to every branch of inquiry
that might, at the time, provoke intellectual
curiosity, with disinterestedness, with assiduity
and with comparatively little emotion. It
was inevitable, perhaps, that this great mind
should be disputed in later generations by
opposing camps, for the profundity of his

observations about knowledge, conduct and the universe being undeniable, philosophers, moralists and critics, too, have been irresistibly tempted to lay exclusive claim to the support of his authority. The Fathers of the Christian Church, and with them Dante, found in his writings a support for Christian dogma : other transcendental philosophers have followed them. Nor did they find him difficult to attach, since his extant writings are fragmentary and not always consistent, and it is a simple matter to interpret his use of Platonic theory more platonically than he intended. And so, on the ground of the incomplete literary treatise known as the *Poetics*, transcendental critics have been unable to keep their hands off Aristotle, attributing to him all kinds of moral vehemences in aesthetic judgments which would certainly have surprised him. The great body of the Platonic dialogues, which more truly are romantic, colour fatally the views of certain minds about Aristotle, who cannot defend himself : and there is something not a little comic in seeing a romanticist critic of to-day, Mr. Middleton Murry, working himself up to a passionate proclamation of Aristotle as the very foundation of moralistic idealism in

criticism.* Personally, I am convinced that
a study of Aristotle's work, including the
Ethics, the *Politics* and the *Posterior Analytics*,
shows this view to be a wrong one. It is
surely nearer the truth to see Aristotle as
Mr. T. S. Eliot sees him.†

" In whatever sphere of interest, he looked
steadily and surely at the object ; in his short
and broken treatise (the *Poetics*) he provides
an eternal example—not of laws, or even of
method, for there is no method except to be
intelligent ; but of intelligence itself swiftly
operating the analysis of sensation to the
point of principle and definition."

A truth, however, emerges from this confusion about Aristotle's attitude in literary
criticism, which is that literary criticism is
not a perfectly appropriate field for the
purely scientific activity. Literature is not
simply a collection of phenomena, nor a system
of logically connected ideas which can be
expressed by unchanging symbols, nor a causal
process of which every step is perceptible :
it is produced by the most recondite processes

* " Aspects of Literature." *The Function of Criticism.*
† " The Sacred Wood." *The Perfect Critic.*

of only casually related human minds and it
is like a marvellous froth thrown up on the
waves of that confused immediacy which we
call earthly life. It is living but it is not simply
organic ; it is ideal but it is not abstract ;
it has purposes but not a single purpose ; it
is expression but it is also experience ; it is
independent of daily life yet it is about men and
women. Moreover, literature has a quality
called beauty, which is not a category of science
at all. The consequence is that the purely
scientific spirit critically projected upon this
confused and complex material finds itself at
a loss, and either tends to sheer away into some
partial view of it in which it finds itself more
at home, or it tends itself to become impure
and to adopt, or seem to adopt, an attitude
of assertion rather than one of inquiry. It
will sheer off, for instance, into the purely
historical investigation of human developments,
into the scholarly discussion of texts and
origins, or into the technical study of method
and form. In these pursuits the scientific
activity may attain useful and practical results,
but its eye is turned away from literature as
a whole and from the essential nature of creative
art. The magic with which art transmutes
experience, the seat and quality of its beauty,

the inevitability of its appeal—these are matters which technical and historical inquiry leaves on one side, or empties them of nearly all their significance. When, on the other hand, it attempts to apply itself to literature as a whole, it either approximates to the creative type of criticism or it lends itself, through being obliged to use unscientific words and ideas, to every kind of misinterpretation. Though it is impossible here further to discuss the *Poetics*, I state my belief that Aristotle, in this attempt to give a purely disinterested account of the best practice in the dramatic poetry of the Attic stage, exposed himself to misunderstandings by having to employ terms charged with fluctuating emotional and moral significances. Where he imagined himself to be using bare terms he seemed to be asserting views, and where he intended to give an accurate account of facts he could be interpreted as laying down precepts.

The difficulty, indeed, is an insoluble one. For the inquiring activity applied to literary criticism the dilemma seems to be absolute : either it must turn away from the essential nature of the very subject which it wishes to examine, or it must cease to be purely scientific. No critic, with the doubtful exception of

Aristotle—and how narrow are the limits of his critical treatise !—has found a way out of the difficulty ; and most of them have slipped off into the safe paths of historical and technical investigation. The libraries of the world are full of their work. The best that can be said of it, even when it applies all the industry, penetration and delicate sensibility which Mr. J. M. Robertson shows in his studies of the Shakespearean canon, is that it arrives at facts, when its deductions are correct : but these facts, however important historically, from the point of view of art are either secondary or irrelevant.

Mr. T. S. Eliot, a creative poet but a sincerely inquiring critic, has faced the difficulty honestly, and it is all the more interesting to observe how short a way he gets towards solving it. His reflections on the subject are to be found in the chapter of his book, " The Sacred Wood," headed *The Perfect Critic*, and in an article on " The Function of Criticism," which appeared in the *Criterion* for October, 1923. He holds that " the end of the enjoyment of poetry is a pure contemplation from which all accidents of personal emotion are removed : thus we aim to see the object as it really is . . . ." This is the kind of statement which

one would expect a mind with a scientific
bias to formulate, in order to give itself a pure
content on which to work : but it would need
a good deal more elucidation before it would
win general acceptance ; indeed, most students
of poetry would repudiate it, and what is
Mr. Eliot to reply ? He can only reply by
scientific proof or an expression of faith, which
is not scientific, that his view is true. So far,
he has not supplied the proof. Having given,
to his own satisfaction, a scientific object
to scientific criticism, he presents criticism
itself as pure knowledge. The defect of most
modern criticism, in his view, is that in default
of knowledge it substitutes emotions for
thoughts. Perfect criticism, which would be
the clear statement of pure knowledge, would
not even need to be dogmatic :

"A precept, such as Horace or Boileau gives
us, is merely an unfinished analysis. It appears
as a law, a rule, because it does not appear in
its most general form ; it is empirical . . . .
The dogmatic critic, who lays down a rule,
who affirms a value, has left his labour incomplete. Such statements may often be justifiable
as a saving of time ; but in matters of great
importance, the critic must not coerce, and he

must not make judgments of worse or better. He must simply elucidate : the reader will form the correct judgment for himself."

We should be grateful to Mr. Eliot for stating the matter so absolutely, and for not concealing the fact that his view of criticism is fundamentally opposed to that of nearly all the literary critics who have ever lived. He therefore illustrates brilliantly the positions into which the scientific mind is forced when it tries to apply itself satisfactorily to an impure material. Mr. Eliot admits that the purely technical critic can only be called a critic in a narrow sense, but he insists that the interpretative critic, even a Coleridge, whom he considers the greatest of English critics, appears to be ruined by his emotions. And it is self-evident that, if you rule emotion out of court, as the scientific spirit is bound to do, these conclusions about the critical literature of the world are necessary corollaries. Besides Aristotle, in fine, Mr. Eliot can only find Remy de Gourmont as another example of a satisfactory " general intelligence " applied to literature : yet even here the question suggests itself whether the real interest of Remy de Gourmont, like that of many analytical French critics, was not, at bottom, psychological rather than literary.

A still more significant thing to be observed is that Mr. Eliot himself is unable to elucidate, so that the reader can judge without further assistance, what in fact is the scientific truth about literature at which the scientific intelligence arrives. Comparing Aristotle and Coleridge, he says : " Everything that Aristotle says illuminates the literature which is the occasion for saying it ; but Coleridge only now and then " : this is true, but it is only a quantitative distinction, not qualitative, as we should expect. We want to know how Aristotle's pure beams differ in quality from Coleridge's impure ones. Mr. Eliot makes a further attempt, the uncompromising sincerity of which attracts sympathy, in the article on the function of criticism. Positing that literature throughout the ages is an orderly and solid whole, which is another way of giving scientific criticism a scientific content, he infers that criticism, " the exposition and commentation of works of art," should be a clear and simple task to be pursued by critics in serious and friendly co-operation. He means—and it is no ignoble idea—that all the critics of the nations should be working for the discovery of critical truth together as, for instance, are all the anatomists and biologists to discover the real functions of the ductless glands. Observing, however, that modern criticism is " no better than a Sunday park of contending and contentious orators," he dismisses all critics, without pausing to consider whether their contentions do not point to some flaw in his own analogy between the objects of science and of criticism, and proceeds to inquire what books, essays, sentences or men have been " useful " in a critical sense. From this he hopes to find a hint of a formula which will express the function of criticism in general. The criticism of an artist in the moment of creation, he finds, is real and useful ; but we do not see it except in the result. Mr. Eliot turns then to written criticism for his formula, and does not find it. Some of the " creative " critics, he observes, may be useful to other writers, but there is no rule, and they are apt to have a poor sense of fact. Fact can be determined by external evidence, but " interpretative " criticism cannot, therefore it is uncertain and unscientific. The only legitimate interpretation, because nothing extraneous is imported by the interpreter, is to put a reader in the possession of facts : to read him poetry, in fine. There are other facts, of course, technical and historical : unfortunately, they vary in relevance, but their chief merit—a sadly negative one—is that they " cannot corrupt taste." They are contained in " innumerable dull and tedious books." Here Mr. Eliot breaks off in gloom. He has found a test for vicious books, namely that these supply " opinion and fancy." For the rest : " For the kinds of critical work which we have admitted, there is the possibility of co-operative activity, with the further possibility of arriving at something outside of ourselves, which may provisionally be called truth. But if anyone complains that I have not defined truth, or fact, or reality, I can only say apologetically that it was no part of my purpose to do so, but only to find a scheme into which, whatever they are, they will fit, if they exist."

This is hardly a stimulating or satisfying conclusion, and the house which Mr. Eliot furnishes for a possible tenancy by reality looks as if it might be distinctly cramped. Nevertheless, his frankness is useful, and enables us to dispense with further comment on the discomfort attending the purely scientific activity in criticism.

The third type of critical predisposition,

to the practical activity, is the normal type of the great bulk of criticism good and bad, which is to be read in the periodical press. It is the type of all human activity at ordinary levels, and it is applied by the good, useful minds of the orders below genius who do most of the world's work, if they do not supply its most lasting ideas. Critics of the practical disposition may share in the creative or scientific impulses, they have style and sensibility in varying degrees, they wish to express and to know : but, with all their individual variations, they agree more or less in leaving philosophy and theory to look after themselves and in regarding criticism as a practical function to be performed to the best of their abilities for the divulgation of art, the instruction of the public, for the making— as Matthew Arnold put it—of an intellectual situation for creation, and for the earning of their living. They are content to have hazy and inarticulate ideas about ultimate things such as the nature of artistic beauty, the absolute criterion, the essential qualities of " permanence," and the texture of absolute critical truth : they are satisfied that from their own studies and discussions they have attained to ideas on these subjects which are generally accepted, and they aim at applying them in successive instances with the consciousness that, in particular, men's tastes inexplicably differ beyond hope of reconciliation. Being unencumbered by too imperiously absolute ideals, they show fewer gaps, if lesser depths, in their appreciations : they will not dismiss sensuous beauty with a shrug or be too impatient with the work of second order. They would rather praise than blame, comment than analyse. Mr. Robert Lynd, one of the most graceful of our modern essayists who carries a charm of style and a genial discursiveness into his appreciations of literature, has expressed more than once this view of the critical activity. For instance, in his "Art of Letters,"* he writes :

" Criticism at its highest is not a theorist's attempt to impose iron laws on writers : it is an attempt to capture the secret of that ' inner light ' and of those who possess it and to communicate it to others. It is also an attempt to define the conditions in which the ' inner light ' has most happily manifested itself, and to judge new writers of promise according to the measure in which they have

* p. 125.

been true to the spirit, though not necessarily to the technicalities, of the great tradition. Criticism, then, is not the Roman father of good writing : it is the disciple and missionary of good writing. The end of criticism is less law-giving than conversion. It teaches not the legalities, but the love, of literature."

Again, in the same volume, his essay on " The Critic as Destroyer " puts cogently with many applications to modern authors, the general theory that

" Criticism, then, is praise, but it is praise of literature. There is all the difference in the world between that and the praise of what pretends to be literature. True criticism is a search for beauty and truth and an announcement of them. It does not care twopence whether the method of their revelation is old or new, academic or futuristic. It only asks that the revelation shall be genuine. It is concerned with form because beauty and truth demand perfect expression. But it is a mere heresy in aesthetics to say that perfect expression is the whole of art that matters. It is the spirit that breaks through the form that is the main interest of criticism."

Many of the terms here are undefined and vague, but the daily work of criticism must rely upon the existence of general consent in their meaning. Mr. Lynd goes farther than some of our practical critics in avowing a personal note in his criticism. He likes to think of the critic, he has said, rather " as a portrait painter than a judge," and that he is not always just to his sitter, his attack on Mr. Eliot* is an instance. He is content to hold that good criticism is " almost any sort of good writing about books by a man or woman of taste,"† and this, in all conscience, is a loose and airy definition. Yet, if his discriminations are not systematic, and if his expression of them is transitory—the task of a day rather than the fruit of a year's reflection—their good sense, their feeling for what is great and beautiful, and their liveliness have done their work in the minds of the readers for whom they were intended; and they have fulfilled that function of criticism upon which Matthew Arnold insisted, of being the disinterested endeavour to learn and to propagate the best that is known and thought in the world.

The revelation of delight is no mean aim,

* " Books and Authors," *Mr. T. S. Eliot as Critic.*
† Ib. p. 267.

even though the principles of delight are allowed
to remain obscure. Praise of the good is a
more powerful engine in correcting taste than
abuse of the bad, and gratitude is a human
virtue none too frequently exercised in favour
of artists. At the end of his "History of
English Criticism," Professor Saintsbury proclaims the same view of criticism, and
naturally, for it has throughout inspired his
extensive labours in the field of literature.
Among critics of the practical disposition he
is the highest type, for his activity is immense
and inexhaustible and his delight, insatiably
sought and enthusiastically recorded, is remarkable in its positiveness and intensity : there
is something gigantic about it, like a gale,
which blows irresistibly through the reader.
If you ask him for ultimate standards he will
not give you them, but he will point to the
lasting masterpieces of literature and say:
" learn these, and you will find your standards
for yourself."

But if some more captious spirit were to
inquire what, after all, was a lasting masterpiece, Mr. J. C. Squire, another champion
among our practical critics, will answer him
as he combats,* without too much conviction,

* " Books Reviewed," *A Critic.*

99

the purely impressionistic theories of criticism
put forward by Jules Lemaitre :

" We may realise how standards change and
how intelligent men differ. But a critic may,
if he choose, still endeavour to make, without
dishonesty, pronouncements which are something more than the records of personal
impressions and judgments which are more
than confessions of taste. Let us rule out the
question of absolute validity ; the fact remains
that mankind has been agreed in designating
as the best literature, that which has retained
humanly speaking, a permanent hold upon
readers. It may quite easily be admitted
that works with many great qualities die young
. . . . the fact remains that in the world in
which critics live and for which they chiefly
write the prime interest of a work of art lies in
its chances of ' lasting.'

" The source of our preoccupation here is
as dark as everything else about us. But,
under that mysterious and menacing cope
we must have our toys, and we may amuse
ourselves with admiring ' immortal ' literature
as well as in any other way, and it *is*
possible, without presumption and without
dreaming of reaching ' infallible ' principles,

to escape to some extent the completely anarchistic and personal attitude of Jules Lemaitre."

Every critic, in fine, has formed some opinion in the course of his practice about the qualities that make for " lasting." We can make certain deductions from our own historical epoch. We feel that some things will live and that others will not, and we may try, if we like to systematise those feelings.

" Works admitted to retain an active life after a hundred, or five hundred, years, may be set apart, sorted, analysed ; and most interesting and valuable results may flow from such a study, powerful weapons given to critics who do feel a little more need for dogmatising than was felt by M. Lemaitre . . . .

All the same, I think we can, after all, leave it to the Germans to do the job thoroughly."

With this humorous and typical reflection we may leave the practical spirit in English criticism to be summed up.

IV

SELF-EXPRESSIVE CRITICS.

At the present moment in England criticism
of the self-expressive, or creative, disposition is
not represented by any very authoritative figure,
nor do its pronouncements sound through the
literary spaces in particularly bell-like tones.
There is no sage,—no Goethe, no Coleridge,
not even a W. E. Henley—at whose feet the
sucking critics sit to imbibe a philosophy or
study an attitude. Professor Saintsbury is
a sage, but not of the prophetic order : what he
expresses is a general delight in literature,
a vast knowledge of books, and certain idiosyn-
cracies of taste which he makes no attempt to
rationalise. Dr. Edmond Gosse is father of the
wits, but he has never attempted to mount the
pulpit ; and Sir Arthur Quiller Couch's
personally conducted tours among the beauties
of literature, though stimulating and splendidly
organised with plenty of amusement by the way,
belong distinctly to the practical activity.
Mr. George Moore, veteran master of prose
form, uses the matter of criticism for the
construction of an intimate kind of social

comedy, in which he himself plays both hero and claque ; but the judgments which contend in his dialogues have only a dramatic, not a critical, significance. And if, in default of sages who by long practice in high endeavour should have won a right to dictate, we turn to the poets and other creative writers, we find that most of them are too busily occupied in writing poems or composing novels to seek self-expression in criticism, though they may write reviews and studies for other purposes. This is a healthy state of affairs, of which no complaint need be made. When it is accepted that one may cram anything into a lyric and everything into a novel, the poet, the novelist, and the dramatist too, are not likely to spill over into the secondary vessel of criticism when the creative impulse is upon them : their criticism, as a rule, is strictly practical in its aim.

Some years ago, it is true, Mr. Lascelles Abercrombie wrote a critical study of Mr. Thomas Hardy which, in spite of revealing a deep poetic sympathy with the Wessex novels, displayed the philosophically rhapsodical weaknesses of " creative " criticism below its best. Since then, however, this poet has left the field of literary criticism to combine the formulation of a completely transcendental aesthetic philosophy with a sober and practical investigation of English prosody. Neither of these endeavours come properly into our perspective, any more than do such entertaining and enlightening confessions as appear in Mr. Robert Graves's "Notes on English Poetry." What then of the prophets? Mr. Wells and Mr. Bernard Shaw, whose works certainly contain brilliant expressions of the critical spirit in creative form, might doubtless, had their inclinations so moved them, have made literary criticism the medium for their disgusts, their aspirations and their sarcasms, just as Mr. G. K. Chesterton has occasionally made it the medium for propaganda of a social and ethical ideal ; but Mr. Chesterton found more promising outlets for the celebration of beer and bigotry as elements of Utopia, and Mr. Wells and Mr. Shaw preferred to impose themselves upon their age in other ways. They are creative critics, indeed, but sociological rather than artistic ; Mr. Thomas Hardy and Mr. Rudyard Kipling have not been moved to emulate Wordsworth in placing revolutionary critical introductions before their works ; and if Mr. Conrad* is now being tempted to imitate Henry James in fitting new prefaces to old

---

* These words were written before his lamented death.

novels, his words of affectionate retrospect are far from being so exciting critically as those passionate hints at secrets of artistic concoction which that other great novelist, in an ecstasy of communicativeness, never quite succeeded in revealing.

In fact, the chief creative artists in contemporary literature do not find in criticism a channel for the creative impulse ; and the leading moralists and philosophers, if we have any, are not critics either. We must therefore be content to see what the critics themselves have to show. The pure impressionists, writers like Mr. Arthur Symons and Mr. Arthur Machen, are examples of a creative impulse in one direction, that of describing beautifully their own mental sensations. Their criticism is not so much criticism as an artful narrative of spiritual adventure, which should come partly under the head of autobiography and partly under that of fiction. But critics like the late Mr. Clutton Brock, Mr. Hugh Fausset and Mr. Middleton Murry, are interesting examples of the creative impulse working through criticism in another direction. And this direction is the formulation of a moral system, or the expression of moral aspirations.

There is no stronger stimulus to self-expression than a really imperious moral impulse, and though the expression of a morality may be effected through any of the creative symbols and images, there is also in it a purely rational element which lends itself to such a mixed medium as criticism. Critics whom a creative impulse leads in this particular direction differ considerably according as the moral intuition is dominating or only accessory, and according as it influences their attention to literature. There are some whom it sweeps right away from the apparent subject, and others whose artistic outlook it just richly colours without seriously altering the perspective.

The formal merits of Mr. Clutton Brock's writings on literature are chiefly artistic. At his best he was a good reflective essayist in the great English tradition, pleasant in manner, graceful in phrase, and endowed with a gift of letting the light play on many facets of a subject: but he was never a great critic. Criticism was not really the activity in which his nature found its ideal outlet, and he is a typical instance of low-powered creative energies which drift into literary criticism as a path of least resistance. It seems to be agreed by those who knew him that he never succeeded in writing the book which should have completely expressed the richness of his faculties, but that he had come nearest to it when morals or religion rather than art or literature had been uppermost in his mind. Certainly, such a book as " The Ultimate Belief " is deeper and more expressive than his amiable essays on books. Clutton Brock was essentially an emotional moralist ; it is not surprising, therefore, to find that, as a critic of literature, he regarded emotion as the final arbiter, and that, since character is a function of moral activity, he was mainly interested in creative literature as an expression, or a revelation, of a human character, rather than of an artistic idea.

" Therefore, in considering what we owe to the genius of Swinburne, we should not ask what ideas we have got from him, but what emotions, and of what nature and strength ; for emotion is the final test of the value of all things."*

" More than philosophy, art tells us the truth ; for the most sincere philosopher tells it consciously, but the artist tells it unconsciously."†

" In the matter of art there are no oughts. The wind bloweth where it listeth."‡

* Essays on Books, p. 64.
† More Essays on Books, p. 8.
‡ Ib. p. 4.

These are typical sentences which show the foundations upon which Clutton Brock built his critical judgments : but he saved himself from the exposure of their instability by avoiding the doubtful cases, by preferring to praise such work as commended itself to his taste—which was sound—rather than conduct critical examinations of good and bad together, and by concentrating most of his critical energy on the exposition of creative art as a revelation of character. A reader who peruses his " Essays on Books " and " More Essays on Books " will receive a considerable amount of aesthetic pleasure and entertainment, but if he proceeds to ask himself to what critical conclusions he has been led, he will have to confess himself at a loss. He will find that he has turned from delight in Shakespeare's characters to admiration of Shakespeare the inspired craftsman who, " living desperately in a hand-to-mouth struggle," yet rose occasionally " from earth to heaven " ; that he has discussed the " attitude " of Dostoievski, Turgenev, Walt Whitman, Vaughan and Marvell to human life in general, observed George Meredith's idiosyncrasies as a writer of novels and poems, and approximated to a reconstruction of Herbert the man and Tolstoy the thinker from the expressions of opinion to be found in their writings ; but that he has seldom had his glance directed on works of art as things in themselves or as related to other works of art, and that, when he is supposed to consider himself out of sympathy with the attitude of an author like Turgenev, he is recommended to obtain more sympathy from some recondite store within him, and not, by any chance, a little more knowledge from a dispassionate study of Turgenev's work. He will have observed that Clutton Brock admired Dickens and Charlotte Bronte very much, but that he admired them as human beings above all, so much so that he devoted a whole essay to vindicating Charlotte's behaviour to Emily. Nearly all Clutton Brock's critical writing shows that an author's work afforded him primarily an approach to an author's personality. It was seldom that he went so near pure criticism as in the chapter in " More Essays on Books " where he points out the defects of English prose or, at least, of the conception of its beauties which Mr. Pearsall Smith conveyed in his " Anthology of English Prose." Seeing that our prose has a distinct tendency to become rhetorical and turgid in moments of excitement, Clutton Brock never did a more useful piece of work than when he insisted that clearness and preciseness should be, and can be, as much virtues of English as of French, and that our poetical prose is only one style, not necessarily the best. On the whole, Clutton Brock's writing about books, tinged as it was with moral and religious yearnings, remained on the level of the agreeably expository, hardly ever stating or clearing up a real critical difficulty. With his belief in the infallibility of emotion and unconsciousness he could not have solved a critical problem if he had raised one, and he was happier when he was suffusing his reflections on life in general with a rich but reasonable idealism. He did not, however, pretend that religion and art were the same, and when he wished to preach a sermon, as not infrequently he did, he did not call it literary criticism.

Mr. Hugh I'Anson Fausset is not so judicious. His work, which is still in a state of development, furnishes a good example of the self-assertive tendency leading criticism astray ; and this misguidance is simply due to a powerful anxiety on his part to identify the whole of ideal good with artistic beauty. His latest book, " Studies in Idealism," expresses with amplitude what is the " self-expression " which, though he also writes poems, he strives to attain through criticism. It is, in fact, the statement of a religion : he calls it the religion of poetry, and it is set forth in the first chapter with an enthusiasm which does him credit and in language which is ardently transcendental. True art, he says, is more reasonable than logic, and more moral than religion.

" True imagination, therefore, is a combination of passionate thought and physical sensation, and its dispositions are absolutely true, because they represent the combined power of life and of thought, the union of creation and perception. Such creative perception is commonly named intuition, and because the reason inherent in it embraces and defines a far wider landscape than logic alone can focus, its rational consistency has been seldom recognised by the narrowly logical."

" The true poet is philosopher, psychologist and moralist, but all to an absolute degree ; above all he is a man spurred on by high passions, championing the deepest and truest values in the face of society and circumstance, and all the grinding logic of the world. His example should serve both to call men back to nature and speed them on to truth. He is no literary manikin tasting the pleasures of cultivated emotions or paddling in the stream of private sensations. He is one with the creative spirit of life, and the world that is and that is to be mingled in his utterance. He is at his highest ' the prophetic soul of the world dreaming on things to come ' ; for the end of the world too is surely beauty."

There is a gustiness about these passages : and there is a sense that the author's emotions are not quite pure—that his spiritual eye rolls in aspiration towards the absolute while his nostrils snort with an ill-concealed indignation against the present. It would be useless, even if it were here possible, to examine calmly so intuitional a view of the universe, its end and the place of the poet in it ; and it may be left to other transcendentalists to take up with Mr. Fausset his slighting attitude towards gods. What he writes about religion, indeed, is not convincing, for he misrepresents both the religious experience and the force of religion as a historical factor. Apart from this, his idealistic formulas are no more objectionable than many others that have gone before : every man's thinking has a share in them. But what is here to the point is to observe that in this little book, which ranges through several centuries of literature, the only criterion adopted is that of philosophic idealism. The author is honest : he calls it the " ideal critical " approach. But the result of this approach is that we consider Shakespeare simply as a moral consciousness evolving from stage to stage of idealistic philosophy, Milton as an exponent of Puritanism purged by a personal paganism, and Wordsworth simply as enunciator of profound moral judgments. Mr. Fausset does not seem to realise the one-sidedness of the effect produced, and his own appearance—to use an expressive neologism—of being hopelessly " viewy " when he writes about literature. Spiritual discontent is not a state of mind to be despised, if it leads to greater spiritual truth ; but, even if an " ideal " approach to literature may legitimately include " viewiness," it cannot possibly be regarded as critical. At best it is historical : " Studies in Idealism " is, in fact, an appendix to a history of philosophy, and its title might well have been " The Evolution of Moral Ideas in Poetry." As such it has some value, though not all its judgments are well-considered : but nowhere can one find in it the critical appreciation of a work of art.

Mr. Fausset himself admits as much when he

remarks of " Absalom and Achitophel " that it is
petty in the light of ideal philosophy but
" satirically, how sublime ! " This form of
sublimity, we infer, is not worth dwelling on.
In the same way the particular perfection that
makes Shakespeare Shakespeare and that which
so sharply distinguishes the gold from the clay
in Wordsworth recede from view when the
attention is exclusively occupied by the celebration of poetry as a specific against " the agony
of spiritual sickness " which admits mankind
to the radiant " health of life lived according
to love." Similarly, it is the assumption of an
uncompromising moral attitude which weakens
Mr. Fausset's " Tennyson." This book contains
many passages of dignified and even beautiful
narration, but the stiff and condemnatory pose
of the author towards Tennyson and his friends,
who " erred in believing that beauty, however
refined and condescendingly human, could also
be true, unless they gave themselves fearlessly
to life," spoils his critical discrimination. It
would be well, parenthetically be it said, if
young idealists of to-day were to be forbidden
to use the word " life " with an actual or
implied capital L : or, whenever they did so,
were compelled to append a footnote explaining
with limpid precision what exactly they meant.

Nowadays, in the hands of the idealists, " life "
is being as much misused as once was " liberty ":
like a cocktail, it can be given all the colours of
the spectrum by a skilled mixer, but all com-
binations produce little more than vague but
warm feelings in the region of the midriff and
an increased volubility. There was a streak
of moral cowardice, possibly, in Tennyson, but
it is not a key to a proper view of all his poetry :
and the amplitude with which Mr. Fausset
illustrates it finds no counterpart in his appreciation of what is individual and poetically
beautiful in Tennyson's work. He is per-
functory in praise, for such beauty is beneath
his austere view. In consequence, it happened
that an ironist, who about the same time took
an interest in Tennyson, gave a better portrait
of man and work than the idealist. Mr. Harold
Nicolson, who was struck by the idea of applying
Mr. Lytton Strachey's biographical methods to
the Victorian poet, and who produced some
disrespectfully comic effects in the application,
did nevertheless suggest—though he failed to
elaborate—where the real poet in Tennyson is
to be found, and pointed out the works which
future   critics   would   have   to   analyse.
Mr. Fausset's portrait of Tennyson was in many
ways more dignified than Mr. Nicolson's, but

it was Mr. Nicolson's which left barbs in the
memory, not only barbs of irony, but pricks
to a truer critical appreciation of the essential
poet in Tennyson. Mr. Nicolson was
disinterested, Mr. Fausset was not : and those
who compare what these two authors have to
say on " Maud," the lyrics in " The Princess "
and " In Memoriam " will see with which state
of mind the spirit of criticism was most at home.
She is a shy spirit, and when she hears her name
boomed from an ethical pulpit to an ethically
thirsty congregation, she slips out unobserved,
long before the ethical congregation, all
unconscious of her departure, have received the
ethical benediction and resumed their
mackintoshes.

The critical work of Mr. Middleton Murry
is upon an altogether different level ; and
perhaps some measure of the difference may be
found in the fact that in one short article on
" The Problem of Keats " (" Aspects of
Literature ") he managed to say all that it took
Mr. Fausset a whole volume to say, and to
say it more impressively. That he takes
a juster view of art's place in the universe may
easily be seen from his essay on " The Function
of Criticism " in the same volume. Here
he says :

" Art is autonomous, and to be pursued for its own sake, precisely because it comprehends the whole of human life ; because it has reference to a more perfectly human morality than any other activity of man ; because, in so far as it is truly art, it is indicative of a more comprehensive and unchallengeable harmony in the spirit of man. It does not demand impossibilities, that man should be at one with the universe or in tune with the infinite ; but it does envisage the highest of all attainable ideals, that man should be at one with himself, obedient to his own most musical law."

This passage, which comes at the conclusion of a discussion which is a very interesting evidence to Mr. Murry's critical impulses, is lucidity itself beside the metaphysical transformation-scenes in which Mr. Fausset involves art : and his critical ability is at once betrayed by his recognition that art is concrete, that the greater the art the more concrete it is, and that the activities of the artist and the critic are not hazy mysteries, nor comparable either to Delphic ecstasy or to the inspired inspection of sacred entrails. He goes on in this essay to lay it down that upon the critic is imposed the solemn responsibility of constructing a hierarchy of literary value :

" But, in regarding the work of art as a thing in itself, he will never forget the hierarchy of comprehension, that the active ideal of art is indeed to see life steadily and see it whole, and that only he has a claim to the title of a great artist whose work manifests an incessant growth from a merely personal immediacy to a coherent and all-comprehending attitude to life. The great artist's work is in all its parts a revelation of the ideal as a principle of activity in human life. As the apprehension of this ideal is more or less perfect, the artist's comprehension will be greater or less. The critic has not merely the right but the duty, to judge between Homer and Shakespeare, between Dante and Milton, between Cézanne and Michel Angelo, Beethoven and Mozart. If the foundations of his criticism are truly aesthetic, he is compelled to believe and to show that among would-be artists some are true artists and some are not, and that among true artists some are greater than others."

Only considerations of space prevent me from supplementing these two quotations by another from the essay on " Poetry and Criticism," also in this volume. The two articles together, make his right—indeed, his claim—to be reckoned among the creative critics unmistakable. Criticism, as he sees it, is as much an activity of art as poetry, and as such, according to the view of literary creation so ably presented in his stimulating lectures on " The Problem of Style," it is originated by a strong and individual emotion caused in the critic. Thus, criticism is properly creative, primarily, in that it recreates in the reader's mind the peculiar emotion roused in the critic by the work of art ; it is creative, secondarily, because it is an expression of value, and, since all value is ultimately moral, it becomes the expression of a complete humanistic philosophy ; it is creative, finally, because it issues, or should do so, in the formulation of a hierarchy of all literary dominations, principalities and powers, drawn up and adequately expounded.

Such a view of criticism is neither mean nor extravagant : but it would hardly be denied that it is likely to be temperamental. A man of sluggish emotions would scarcely formulate it, certainly not so eloquently as Mr. Middleton Murry has done. In fact, a proper appreciation of his critical virtues, which are very high, and a just view of the imperfections which occasionally mar them, depends on recognising that the dominating contemporary influences that have shaped his work are, in the first place, his own profoundly emotional temperament and, in the second, the repulsion exercised on that temperament by all that has happened to the human mind and polity in the last ten years. Like his poetry, some of his critical essays are passionate championings of higher ideals against baser, and others are profound and painful gropings in the depths of a still uncertain soul. It is, of course, impossible to speak with finality of a literary work that is incomplete. What is here written of Mr. Middleton Murry as a critic is written of the past, and of the future who can speak ? It appears, for the moment, as if he had abandoned criticism to interest himself, through his monthly magazine, " The Adelphi," in an intuitional rejuvenation of morality, in which he figures as the *chela* of Mr. D. H. Lawrence, the *yogi*. However, it is likely that criticism was never a purely self-chosen activity on his part, but imposed by economic necessity on one who would rather have been a journeyman poet than a master-critic. The poetic impulse then, the religious impulse now—those are the fundamental

Murry. These impulses, which are very closely related, found outlet for a time in criticism : one day, as I cannot avoid hoping, they may return to it spontaneously and give to English letters at least the book on Shakespeare which would remove the present disproportion between Mr. Murry's critical performance and his critical talent. A youthful study of Dostoievsky, three volumes of critical essays and the six lectures on " Style "—that is the extent of his critical baggage. Yet, though his commentary on great literature is disconnected and fragmentary, having been too often dictated by mere occasion, though his ethical aesthetic is still but spasmodically formulated, and though he is far, very far, from having arrived at that hierarchy which, he asserts, it is the worthy critic's duty to produce, there is enough to support the judgment that, with all his occasionally childish petulances, his somewhat solemn over-emphases, and his frequent failure to achieve beauty in his own prose, he has—or must we write " had " ?—a critical mind of the very first order, comparable, at its brightest, to that of a Coleridge.

As a critic Mr. Middleton Murry has already earned, if not popularity, certainly respect and admiration among the general literary public :

but awe is mixed with this respect. He has
the reputation of being severe and intellectual :
the term " highbrow " has often been thrown
at him, notably by defenders of Georgian poetry
of which he was apt to be contemptuous.
This view of him is intelligible, on a superficial
view, but is easily seen to be in the main
untrue. Possibly, he was unjust to certain
poets with whose poetical outlook he had no
instinctive sympathy : besides, the criticism
of current literature, unless peculiarly suited to
his own mood, seems to have irked him always.
As he wrote in the essay " A Critical Credo "
(" Countries of the Mind ") :

" Putting a valuation upon new books is
perhaps the least valuable, as it is certainly the
most dangerous, part of criticism. It is almost
impossible for a literary critic to be really sincere
in dealing with contemporary production."

Moreover, one of his imperfections is a tendency to use contorted and stilted language
when struggling with particular intensity to
express an elusive idea. Such language suggests
the schoolmaster, but it does not make the
highbrow. Mr. T. S. Eliot *is* a highbrow,
and writes with an admirable limpidity. But,

in reality, it is a proof of how little average
brains are exercised that it was possible for some
apparently Olympian frowns, some coldness to
successful poets and a few rather heavy words
such as " explication," " organic " and
" governance " to win Mr. Middleton Murry
the title of intellectual—even though he called
himself one—when nearly every page of his
writing shows vehement emotion jogging the
intellect's elbow, or guiding its pencil, as Alice
in the story guided that of the White King.
It was emotion—not, of course, a raw emotion,
but one refined through much reflection and
ministered to by an almost torturing sense of
spiritual beauty—that really inspired his
judgments on poetry just after the war, no
less than his poem " Cinnamon and Angelica,"
which had much sad beauty. In the volume
" Aspects of Literature," the deeply sympathetic articles on the poetry of Edward
Thomas and G. M. Hopkins and on the letters
of Charles Sorley balance those less sympathetic
on Mr. Masefield, Mr. Yeats and on " The
Present Condition of English Poetry." Just as
the repudiation in Sorley's letters of the gallant
and Rupert Brookeish attitude to war moved
him to passionate acquiescence, so the peculiar,
poignant quality of Edward Thomas's overtones

moved him, not only to beautiful language, but to prove that he indeed had, as few others of his day, the supreme critical gift of clearly expressing and conveying all the peculiar quality which he felt.

Moreover, in the article on " The Present Condition of English Poetry "—which was a needlessly pompous title to give to a review of a volume of " Georgian Poetry " and a volume of " Wheels "—in the middle of the somewhat slighting moderation with which Mr. Middleton Murry appraised some of the poets of the day, in a tone unintentionally a little donnish, there suddenly bursts out that uncontrollable personal emotion of his in a greeting of Wilfred Owen's poem "Strange Meeting " which is almost embarrassing to readers who do not happen to get from it that particular emotion. Mr. Murry found in that poem, at that time, " an awe, an immensity, an adequacy to that which has been most profound in the experience of a generation." What he means is clear, but it is equally clear that this is not the last word of criticism, though one feels that at the time when he wrote them he would have defended his words with his last breath. Adequacy to a particular experience, after all, is a very

strange critical standard of art, and would be
unlikely to commend itself to any critic whose
own experience was not of a poignant kind.
It appears again when Mr. Murry writes of
Mr. Thomas Hardy's lyrical poems :

" We have read these poems of Thomas
Hardy, read them not once, but many times.
Many of them have already become part of
our being ; their indelible impress has given
shape to dumb and striving elements in our
soul ; they have set free and purged mute,
heart-devouring regrets. And yet, though
this is so, the reading of them in a single
volume, the submission to their movements
with a like unbroken motion of the mind,
gathers their greatness, their poignancy and
passion, into one stream, submerging us and
leaving us patient and purified.

There have been many poets among us in the
last fifty years, poets of sure talent, and it may
be even of genius, but no other of them has
this compulsive power. The secret is not
hard to find. Not one of them is adequate
to what we know and have suffered. We
have in our hearts a new touchstone of poetic
greatness. We have learned too much to be
wholly responsive to less than an adamantine

honesty of soul and a complete acknowledgment of experience. 'Give us the whole,'
we cry, 'give us the truth.' Unless we can
catch the undertone of this acknowledgment,
a poet's voice is in our ears hardly more than
sounding brass or a tinkling cymbal."

This is Mr. Murry in one of his most aggrava-
ting moods, of sonorous and rather hectoring
monologue, in which he insists on speaking of
his own emotions and the reflections which
they suggest to him as general and undeniable.
The reader is antagonised because he knows
that all the momentous feelings and reactions
in which " we " are assumed to be involved
are, in fact, only applicable to one individual ;
and that the passage is less criticism than
rhapsody. But it is perfectly obvious that
Mr. Murry does not really mean to be hectoring
and to convey the impression that those who
do not think thus are mean and grubby souls ;
nor is he really doing the critic's work of
assessing Mr. Hardy for all time or putting
him into a hierarchy : he is trying to respond
to the intense emotions which the poems have
aroused in him. He is yearning, also, to impose
a view of Mr. Hardy on a possibly recalcitrant
or neglectful generation. Heaven forbid that

a writer should be chidden for expressing admiration, especially so worthy an admiration as this! But the fault here is that intensity of feeling leads Mr. Murry to base critical admiration on grounds that are not universal, just as, in another instance, it leads him to a general statement for which he has none but an emotional justification: " Tchehov is a standard by which modern literary effort must be measured, and the writer of prose or poetry who is not sufficiently single-minded to apply the standard to himself is of no particular account."

I have given examples of the good and the bad in Mr. Murry's critical predisposition and tried to show that it is anything but coldly intellectual: but I should do him a serious wrong if I did not express the conviction that the good far outweighs the bad. The essays on Hardy's lyrics and on Tchehov, though they contain infelicities, seize these two great artists in flashes of vision and hold them for a moment transfigured as symbols of the eternal in beauty. When the flash is over, one may ask the questions which have not been answered, but the memory of its dynamic power remains to stimulate the mind. The great thing was to have the flash, even if the attendant emotions were almost too much for the critical intelligence and the ecstasy of the energumen clouded the self-control of the writer. The chief thing is to give thanks for an actual good when one finds it : and the actual good of Mr. Murry's criticism, its peculiar excellence beyond all the secondary virtues of taste and knowledge which are his, is this unusually intense vibration of emotional sensibility, which sometimes lifts him up as on the wing of some mountain-dwelling bird, though at other times it makes his utterance harsh and obscure. The fault is the price which imperfect human nature pays for the virtue : and it is interesting to observe that in the calmer mood which the volume " Countries of the Mind " reflects, the virtue remains and the fault is attenuated. In this volume we have the beautiful little discourse on " Shakespeare and Love," and the appreciations of Amiel and of Doughty's " Arabia Deserta " : it is only to be regretted that no volume yet contains that article on " The Nature of Poetry " published in *The Times* Literary Supplement during October, 1922, which, if any were to question the value of creative criticism, would be a sufficient answer. To a mind like Mr. T. S. Eliot's it may seem to be beyond

question that " the end of the enjoyment of
poetry is a pure contemplation from which
all the accidents of personal emotion are
removed " ; but this is not the last word,
either. Mr. Middleton Murry's emotions,
which are of the kind that vibrate to the
essential quality of the greatest things, seem
to catch the ethereal elements in poetic beauty
with more ease than Mr. Eliot's contemplations.

Mr. Eliot, it is true, might point with a
smile to the fact that for sheer realisation
of the essentially critical function as well as
for grace of literary expression, two essays of
Mr. Murry's, those on Collins and John Clare
—possibly one might add the penetrating but
controversial essay on Flaubert—where his
emotions were not very deeply engaged, are
precisely the most worthy to be included in
an anthology of criticism.* Yet it is the
creative spirit which suffuses the essays with a
graceful flush of life : they are not inquiries,
but expressions of serenely arrived-at con-
victions, not exasperated by the sense of
conflict or overloaded with ecstasy. The
essay on Collins, in particular, is a brilliant
and delicate piece of analysis, showing the
gradual preparation of a less exalted spirit for

* All in the volume, " Countries of the Mind."

the one great moment when, like some lower peak in an Alpine sunset, it was transfigured in the ray of absolute poetry : its structure and its language are alike admirable, and possibly, as a pure work of critical art, it is the highest achievement of its author. At the same time, these essays do not reveal as others less perfect do the hot, but sombre and often smoky, flame which burns at the heart of his work. Mr. Middleton Murry is a crusader by temperament, and what he is crusading against is a cold, mechanistic view of reality, cynicism in politics, determinism in morals and what he calls the fiat of logic in art. That is why he is disrespectful to Benedetto Croce and why he repudiates classicism ; he fears in them deadening influences, tending to wrap up the free and glorious individual in the cerecloths of categories and traditions. Mere sensuous beauty, on the other hand, the poetry that is turned out like the shapely vase by the skilful potter, seems to him unworthy of much attention. Only with an effort, as in his review of Mr. Walter de la Mare's poems, can he focus his critical attention at all patiently on contemporary art, however beautiful, which lingers in by-paths or seems to escape life by an enchantment. Great literature

for him must be in the main current of
life, and what he considers to be the process
by which great poetry comes into being can best
be studied in the fourth and fifth lectures on
" Style." Though they miss limpidity and
their thought is uncomfortably condensed,
these two chapters are a work of which no critic
need be ashamed, and they reveal a mind which,
however strongly emotions and aspirations
dominate it, is unusually well equipped to
probe the secrets and interpret the beauties
of literary art at its highest. This little book
has had no sequel : other interests have super-
vened. The poet and the idealist in him gave
him his peculiar quality as a critic and now
have driven the critic into fields, like
Nebuchadnezzar. If the critic returns, the
kind of book which we shall be expecting will
be some rival to that model of philosophical
criticism, Professor Santayana's " Three
Philosophical Poets."

V

SCIENTIFIC CRITICS

MR. MIDDLETON MURRY boldly writes down all
great writers since Rousseau Romantics and
proclaims Romanticism as the principle of life
in art, rejecting Classicism as the principle of
death. We need not be too much perturbed.
There are moments when for the ardent-
minded it becomes imperative to play at the
game of labels. Banners and drums inspire
marchers. No great harm is done, though the
permanent good is not obvious. Nevertheless,
it is a mistake to suppose that in criticism the
writer who is creative in a philosophical sense
need be a Romanticist, one who believes, in
Professor Santayana's words, that "he creates
a new heaven and a new earth with each
revolution in his moods or in his purposes."
Professor Santayana is himself a case of an
unromantic philosophical critic ; and there is
a paragraph in his noble essay on Lucretius
("Three Philosophical Poets") which leads
directly to a view of criticism which is not
idealistic :—

"Lucretius, a poet of universal nature,

studied everything in its truth. Even moral
life, though he felt it much more narrowly and
coldly than Wordsworth did, was better understood and better sung by him for being seen in
its natural setting. It is a fault of idealists to
misrepresent idealism, because they do not view
it as a part of the world. Idealism *is* a part of
the world, a small and dependent part of it.
It is a small and dependent part even in the life
of men. This fact is nothing against idealism
taken as a moral energy . . . . But it is the
ruin of idealism taken as a view of the central
and universal power in the world . . . . Nature,
for the Latin poet, is really nature. He loves
and fears her, as she deserves to be loved and
feared by her creatures. Whether it be a wind
blowing, a torrent rushing, a lamb bleating,
the magic of love, genius achieving its purpose,
or a war, or a pestilence, Lucretius sees everything in its causes, and in its total career. One
breath of lavish creation, one iron law of change,
runs through the whole, making all things kin
in their inmost elements and in their last end."

It is an analogous view of literary art which
commends itself to the inquiring predisposition
in criticism. The " one breath of lavish
creation " and the " one iron law of change "

are just the things that interest the scientific critic. He does not wish to recreate wonder or to tabulate the merits of the wonder-workers : he sees the works of human art before him, as Lucretius saw the works of nature, and he wishes to see " everything in its causes." Mr. T. S. Eliot has put this point of view with remarkable force in the essay *Tradition and the Individual Talent* (" The Sacred Wood "). The very simplicity of his language makes his idea a little difficult of apprehension and, as regards its implications, a great deal is left to be filled in by the reader : indeed, it is to be doubted whether in this instance, Mr. Eliot is not a long way short of that complete critical " elucidation " of his which should make the reader's drawing of conclusions so simple a matter. The whole essay, however, will bear reading more than once, and fragmentary quotation does it less than justice : the following passage, however, in itself, is clear and comprehensive :—

" No poet, no artist of any art, has his complete meaning alone. His significance, his appreciation is the appreciation of his relation to the dead poets and artists. You cannot value him alone ; you must set him, for contrast and

134

comparison, among the dead . . . . What happens when a new work of art is created is something that happens simultaneously to all the works of art which preceded it. The existing monuments form an ideal order among themselves, which is modified by the introduction of the new (the really new) work of art among them. The existing order is complete before the new work arrives ; for order to persist after the supervention of novelty, the *whole* existing order must be, if ever so slightly, altered ; and so the relations, proportions, values of each work of art toward the whole are readjusted ; and this is conformity between the old and the new. Whoever has approved this idea of order, of the form of European, of English literature, will not find it preposterous that the past should be altered by the present as much as the present is directed by the past."

Not all critics of the scientific disposition have views so definite and logical on the nature of their subject-matter, but it is worth while realising, from this instance, that criticism of this kind need not be confined to piecemeal dissection, minute research or mere technical investigation, since, on the testimony of so unimpassioned a writer as Mr. Eliot, it may rest upon a view of art which is in its own way mystic, if hardly ecstatic. The truth is, of course, that good critics reach valuable conclusions whether they be primarily romantic, classic, creative, scientific or practical. Moreover, in actual practice, what seems to matter more than the critical predisposition or the critic's fundamental view of art is his personal absorption in his particular subject. It is this, rather than anything peculiarly efficacious in his method of approach, which gives value to the work of the inquiring, or scientific, critic.

Let us take, for instance, the literary criticism of Mr. Lytton Strachey. There is, of course, a strong creative streak in this critical mind which, to the general admiration, has produced the dramatic and historical characters that act their parts so exquisitely in his biographies : but as a literary critic—which he has only spasmodically been—he is of the inquiring and classical disposition. He can speak forcibly of the " craving, which has seized upon our poetry and our criticism ever since the triumph of Wordsworth and Coleridge, at the beginning of the last century, for metaphysical stimulants " ; and in a passage which deserves to be thoroughly pondered by metaphysicals he

effectively protests against the view that a poet
can be tested by his view of life :

" Is it possible to test a poet's greatness by
the largeness of his ' view of life ' ?   How wide,
one would like to know, was Milton's ' view of
humanity ' ?   And, though Wordsworth's sense
of the position of man in the universe was far
more profound than Dante's, who will venture
to assert that he was the greater poet ?   The
truth is that we have struck here upon a
principle which lies at the root . . . . of an
entire critical method—the method which
attempts to define the essential elements of
poetry in general, and then proceeds to ask of
any particular poem whether it possesses these
elements, and to judge it accordingly.   How
often has this method been employed, and how
often has it proved disastrously fallacious !
For, after all, art is not a superior kind of
chemistry, amenable to the rules of scientific
induction.   Its component parts cannot be
classified and tested, and there is a spark within
it which defies foreknowledge . . . . It is the
business of the poet to break rules and to baffle
expectation ; and all the masterpieces in the
world   cannot   make   a   precedent.   Thus
Mr. Bailey's attempts to discover, by quotations

from Shakespeare, Sophocles and Goethe, the qualities without which no poet can be great, and his condemnation of Racine because he is without them, is a fallacy in criticism. There is only one way to judge a poet, as Wordsworth, with that paradoxical sobriety so characteristic of him, has pointed out—and that is, by loving him." *

There is nothing cold or mechanical in this conception of criticism ; in fact, it is partly a well-stated objection to the ultra-scientific conception of literature. Nevertheless, the main weight of its attack is against a false idealism, for Mr. Strachey himself is a critic of the realistic or classical type, all for unimpassioned inquiry and plain statement. Until his " Queen Victoria " he did not, certainly, give a strong impression of loving the object of his historical study : indeed, in " Eminent Victorian " his emotion, one felt, came nearer to what is the next best thing to love, that is, hate. But in his literary criticism it is his power of illuminating the things he loves without rant or fustian but simply by lifting away veils of misunderstanding that makes his " Landmarks of French Literature "

* " Books and Characters," *Racine.*

a permanent contribution to English letters and gives a sense of exceptional achievement to some of the essays collected under the title "Books and Characters." Since what Mr. Strachey most loves in literature is the classical, it is not strange that his mind should have been attracted to French literature, in which the classical has attained such purity and intensity. He speaks uncertainly when his subject is Shakespeare, nor is he very profound— but it was in 1906—when he writes of Blake. On the other hand, when it is a question of defending Racine against mistaken criticism or of analysing the art of Stendhal, he exercises the critic's function with an ease and a mastery that make a deep impression on the reader. The essay on Racine, the very one from which I have quoted above the condemnation of metaphysical criticism, moved one of our creative, idealistic critics to expressions of rapture which were almost excessive ; yet, calmly considered, this essay, as a piece of argument varied by many graces but directed inflexibly to its end and as an instance of understanding opening window after window upon the gloom of stupidity, is nearly perfect. From the supposititious Racine with whom Mr. Strachey begins, cold, artificial, stilted, monotonous, the Racine of many an Englishman, emerges under his potent critical spell another Racine, warm, genuine, with a voice of subtle charm and infinite variety, and above all an idealist embodying the very forms of human life divested of all that is gross and accidental. And this admirable performance is accomplished, in the main, in the strictly classical spirit. I say " in the main," because, towards the end, an intuitional criterion, abhorred by the classical spirit, seems to be hovering on the margin. The situation is saved, however, by an appeal, not directly to the emotions, but to the delicate ear, attuned early to French harmonies ; and secure in his ear, which is a safe material fact, Mr. Strachey can end up with a coda brilliantly scored for trumpets :

" To hear the words of Phèdre spoken by the mouth of Bernhardt, to watch, in the culminating horror of crime and of remorse, of jealousy, of rage, of desire, of despair, all the dark forces of destiny crowd down upon that great spirit, when the heavens and the earth reject her, and Hell opens, and the terrific urn of Minos thunders and crashes to the ground— that indeed is to come close to immortality, to plunge shuddering through infinite abysses, and to look, if only for a moment, upon eternal light."

No trumpets of doubtful validity, however, intrude into the study entitled " Henri Beyle," which is a finished example of criticism calm and elucidatory. Mr. Middleton Murry treated the same subject in " Countries of the Mind " ; and I think it will be agreed by most readers who compare the two essays that both for richness of content and precision of statement the classical critic, on this occasion, surpasses the romantic. Stendhal gives an equal chance to both, owing to his peculiar double-facedness ; both are interested, both apply their methods, and both come to conclusions ; and the salient fact is that Mr. Strachey's interest seems the keener, his method the surer and his conclusions the more convincing. The main reason for his success is, probably, that his love was the greater : had the object of study been Tolstoy, Rousseau or Baudelaire the superiority might have been on the other side. At all events, while Mr. Middleton Murry arrives at a somewhat bare view of Stendhal as a " tragic realist " and as " the smallest of great men," Mr. Strachey, after acutely comparing the position of Stendhal in France to that of Shelley in England, as a personification of national qualities in excess, illuminates, first, Beyle's dry accuracy of style and his psychological precision, pointing out that " Beyle's method " is the classical method—" the method of selection, of omission, of unification, with the object of creating a central impression of supreme reality," and that he wrote like a brilliant talker giving a rapid sketch of vast events to an intelligent audience ; and then, just as the reader is getting impatient of Beyle the pure classic, he shows him as infected with " the virus of modern life—that new sensibility, that new passionateness which Rousseau had first made known to the world, and which had won its way over Europe behind the thunder of Napoleon's artillery." Mr. Strachey briefly but brilliantly brings out all the elements of this dualism, the surgical genius with which mental action is laid bare, the fondness for melodrama, the economy of words when dissection is toward, the exasperating eloquence of the *sentiment d'honneur,* the self-assertiveness, the inconsistency. His " Henri Beyle " is avowedly a portrait of a man rather than a critical study, and as a literary portrait painter Mr. Strachey has few rivals : but there is literary criticism of the best kind in this essay ; and, seeing the scarcity of scientific critics—though investigators of detail are many—one is often tempted to regret that Mr. Strachey's ironic curiosity has not been given a freer run in the fields of English literature.

A similar regret might reasonably be expressed by the lover of letters who compared Mr. T. S. Eliot's exiguous critical performance with the high interest of his critical principles and the power of his critical expression when exercised upon a congenial subject. For some minds, it is true, there is something repellent in the cold lucidity of his critical prose as there is in the equally cold want of lucidity that distinguishes his poem " The Waste Land." Mr. Eliot well remarked of Blake : " He approached everything with a mind unclouded by current opinions. There was nothing of the superior person about him. This makes him terrifying." In this sense he himself, though unclouded by current opinion, is not terrifying, for his mental *hauteur* is pronounced. One is given the impression while reading " The Sacred Wood " of an elect mind writing consciously for the elect, and a certain reaction supervenes against the assumption of this attitude. Even his conception of the pure enjoyment of poetry is esoteric and exclusive :

" There are, for instance, many scattered lines and tercets in the *Divine Comedy* which are capable of transporting even a quite uninitiated reader . . . . to an impression of overpowering beauty. This impression may be so deep that no subsequent study and understanding will intensify it. But at this point the impression is emotional ; the reader in the ignorance which we postulate is unable to distinguish the poetry from the emotional state aroused in himself by the poetry, a state which may be merely an indulgence of his own emotions. The poetry may be an accidental stimulus. The end of the enjoyment of poetry is a pure contemplation from which all the accidents of personal emotion are removed ; thus we aim to see the object as it really is and find a meaning for the words of Arnold. And without a labour which is largely a labour of the intelligence, we are unable to attain that stage of vision *amor intellectualis Dei*."

He speaks with contempt of emotional people such as " stockbrokers, politicians and men of science " ; he finds that " very few treat art seriously " ; he alludes to " the few people who talk intelligently about Stendhal, Flaubert and James " ; and he annoys Mr. Robert Lynd by criticising rather coldly Professor Murray's versions of Euripides and by finding *Hamlet* " most certainly an artistic failure." Indeed, Mr. Eliot is not generous, especially to the art and enthusiasms of the present, but it is bad criticism merely to be annoyed with him instead of inquiring how near he comes to the truth.

The two chapters of " The Sacred Wood " which annoyed Mr. Lynd are not really suitable targets for displeasure. In a too brief discussion of *Hamlet* Mr. Eliot makes perfectly clear what his view is, namely that the play is puzzling and imperfect, judged by the standard of absolute artistic completeness, because it was an unsuccessful attempt to embody " intractable material," some intense but inarticulate emotion for which the poet found no adequate external symbol. One may agree or disagree, but it is a solid and interesting piece of argument. As for Professor Murray's verse translations of Euripides, it is hard to understand how anybody who really loves the Greek language and Euripides could disagree with Mr. Eliot's criticisms of these Swinburnian transformations. It is only fair to admit that in his criticisms,

however deficient in generosity his feelings may
be, Mr. Eliot is never trivial nor beside the
point. He wastes neither time nor words.
His criticisms of critical work, from Swinburne's
to Mr. Irving Babbitt's, are admirably brief and
telling, and they are not unjust. His essay on
" The Possibility of a Poetic Drama," for all
the icy clearness of its language, seldom falls
short of the truth : only at the end does
Mr. Eliot add a touch of vinegar :—

" . . . . our problem should be to take a form
of entertainment, and subject it to the process
which should leave it a form of art. Perhaps
the music-hall comedian is the best material.
I am aware that this is a dangerous suggestion to
make. For every person who is likely to
consider it seriously there are a dozen toymakers
who would leap to tickle aesthetic society into
one more quiver and giggle of art debauch.
Very few treat art seriously. There are those
who treat it solemnly, and will continue to
write poetic pastiches of Euripides and
Shakespeare ; and there are others who treat
it as a joke."

" The Sacred Wood " contains comparatively
few pieces of extended criticism, even in the

literary period wherein Mr. Eliot is most at home, the Elizabethan. The " Notes on the blank verse of Christopher Marlow " bear witness to a well-tuned ear, yet they are but notes ; and the essay on *Hamlet* is little more. Clearly Mr. Eliot, although on his own view " the great bulk of the work of criticism could be done by minds of second order, and it is just these minds of second order that are difficult to find," does not regard himself as called upon to exercise the functions of a critic continuously. How good a critic he can be is shown by his essays on Ben Jonson and Massinger, which are admirable analyses performed with a certainty of aim that comes only from long study and continuous reflection. They vindicate by illustration their author's austere view of the critical method—the application of pure intelligence, the exclusion of emotion, the orderly arrangement of perceptions and so forth—yet the reader is aware throughout of a distinct intellectual enthusiasm. The essay on Massinger is particularly informative and cogent, and the comparisons drawn in the first two or three pages of its second section are remarkable instances of economical and discriminating statement.

Mr. Eliot's criticism is most efficacious when

directed upon some poet who wrote within a tradition : among " whigs " and *illuminés* he confesses himself out of his element without, perhaps, acknowledging the want of elasticity shown thereby in his critical equipment. It is interesting, as an illustration of this, to compare his essays on Swinburne and Blake. Of Swinburne it is amazing how much Mr. Eliot contrives to say in six short pages, in which an ingenious paradox is presented that Swinburne's work is unreal, but perfectly living and indestructible, because it never pretended to be reality and is, in fact, simply language uprooted and blossoming by itself in an " independent life of atmospheric nourishment." ˙ Mr. Eliot, in fine, considers Swinburne a poet of considerable dimensions but unimportant, and one cannot avoid the suspicion that Swinburne's sense of tradition was the saving grace that preserved him from severer condemnation. Over Blake, on the other hand, he can only reflect with melancholy, though with a certain relish too, that a tradition or even a satisfactory mythology might have made a great classic poet out of a man of genius. Mr. Eliot does not here enlarge our knowledge or appreciation of Blake ; on the other hand, he is not, as convinced Romanticists might suppose, merely being tiresome. What he regrets is not that no critical Inquisition existed to stifle Blake's originality, but that he found no convenient channel of traditional belief or legend in which to run off his supernaturalism. As it was—and who can doubt it ?—Blake wasted half his energy in inventing a preposterous theology of which Mr. Eliot writes with some justice :

" And about Blake's supernatural territories, as about the supposed ideas that dwell there, we cannot help commenting on a certain meanness of culture. They illustrate the crankiness, the eccentricity, which frequently affects writers outside the Latin traditions, and which such a critic as Arnold should certainly have rebuked. And they are not essential to Blake's inspiration."

Here and in the passage which follows it Mr. Eliot denies no excellence to Blake which is rightly his, but only suggests what might have been under another dispensation. It would be ridiculous to remain obstinately exasperated with criticism of this kind because one happens to throw up one's hat for the Reformation, Puritanism, the dispensation which produced Blake, Blake's tremendous vapourings and the

individual's right in general to recreate truth
and beauty for himself *ab ovo*. Not all minds
are happy when their environment is formless
or find encouragement in a vast inane. More
than one talent of to-day could be named which
would be producing art of far greater intensity
if it were not compelled, albeit unconsciously,
to waste much of its energy on manufacturing
its own atmosphere and presuppositions, in
making fruitless experiments, and in chasing the
attention of an audience by extravagances
instead of it receiving it as a right for its peculiar
proprieties. The value of tradition, when it is
generally recognised and respected, as it
certainly is not now in England or America,
is that it minimises the need for this expenditure
of energy. It was, after all, not only Dante who
benefited by the existence of a tradition :
Shakespeare and all the Elizabethans benefited,
so did Milton and so did Pope. Mr. Eliot, in
his essay on Dante, brings out forcibly the
supreme importance to so comprehensive a poet
of a philosophy, a religion and mythology which
he could adopt, without discussion, as a frame-
work for his gigantic representations. And those
who will not take Mr. Eliot's word for it, may
find much the same point of view expressed
with more circumstance, eloquence and glow in

Professor Santayana's "Three Philosophical Poets." The difference between the two is the difference between bare truth and truth with feeling : and if truth with feeling appear the more convincing, this, perhaps, is the fundamental criticism of Mr. Eliot's theories. To exclude emotion from the criticism of art seems to be no less arbitrary than to exclude logic : and if Mr. Eliot really wishes to do so, may it not only be a temperamental reaction on his part against excessive emotionalism in others ?

At the same time, it is worth while for the would-be critic, or for any interested reader, to study in the second half of his essay, *Tradition and the Individual Talent*, Mr. Eliot's development of the view which he sums up in the statement that "the emotion of art is impersonal." A careful comparison of this essay with Mr. Middleton Murry's fourth and fifth lectures on "The Problem of Style" is stimulating and profitable. Both use a scientific simile to explain their conception of poetic creation, and it is, perhaps, an ironical testimony to the value of scientific language as an adjunct to the criticism of art that there is nothing to choose between Mr. Murry's exposition of style as "crystallization" and Mr. Eliot's image of the poet's mind as a "catalyst" in whose presence two gases spontaneously combine. The two images are equally suggestive, illustrate diametrically opposite views and when confronted with one another collapse like pasteboard champions. But that is a small matter : the main point is to observe how closely the two critics, who really understand the nature of great art, come when they are probing its fundamental character.

"If you compare several representative passages of the greatest poetry you see how great is the variety of types of combination, and also how completely any semi-ethical criterion of ' sublimity ' misses the mark. For it is not the ' greatness,' the intensity, of the emotions, the components, but the intensity of the artistic process, the pressure, so to speak, under which the fusion takes place that counts."

These words of Mr. Eliot's and those that immediately follow them could almost be fused themselves with Mr. Murry's telling analysis of a passage in *Antony and Cleopatra** as a supreme instance of complete crystallisation. What the Classicist is really attacking—and he

* In " The Problem of Style."

has to admit it—is a metaphysical view of personality which appeals to the Romanticist. Thinking without pride of the individual, he will not have the poet regarded as having a personality to express, for, as he very truly remarks, personal emotions are often neither remarkable nor interesting. He will have it, rather, that the poet is, or has, a medium in which experiences and feelings combine in peculiar ways. " Poetry," he says, " is not a turning loose of emotion, but an escape from emotion ; it is not the expression of personality, but the escape from personality." In a sense these words are true : in another sense, if the phrases were exactly reversed, they would also be true. The great transforming emotion of a poet is hardly comparable to the little emotions of every day, and the artistic personality of the poet is not the historic personality of the man. The supreme effort of artistic creation is both an escape and an expression, but we cannot focus our eyes simultaneously on both these aspects. The solution of the problem seems to lie in recognising them both. To speak of an impersonal emotion is to speak of something which, if it exist, is beyond our experience : it would be better, surely, to call the emotion of great poetry universal, and on that basis the gulf between the Classic and Romantic views of art might possibly be spanned.

To return, however, to the purely inquiring spirit in criticism, there is a distinctly original instance of its virtues to be found in Mr. Percy Lubbock's book " The Craft of Fiction," which appeared in 1921. Since that date its author has been drawn away to more creative enterprises in literature, which have gained him well-deserved recognition as a finished writer of English prose. The elaborate reminiscences of " Earlham," and the closer approach to fiction in " Roman Pictures," with the intricate music of their style, have proved that in the hands of this disciple the tradition of Henry James is anything but a lifeless thing. Mr. T. S. Eliot in his introduction to " The Sacred Wood " imagines, in passing, what a great critic might have done had he applied himself to the study of fiction :

" How astonishing it would be, if a man like Arnold had concerned himself with the art of the novel, had compared Thackeray with Flaubert, had analysed the work of Dickens, had shown his contemporaries exactly why the author of *Amos Barton* is a more *serious* writer than Dickens, and why the author of *La Chartreuse de Parme* is more serious than either ! "

This setting up of the criterion of " seriousness " shows again how mystical is Mr. Eliot for all his intellectualism. In Mr. Lubbock's book, however, we have a concrete instance of a delicately inquiring mind, endowed with sensibility and wide knowledge, applied to the novel as a form of art ; and nothing so general or ethical as " seriousness " arises at any time. It is a most admirable piece of work performed exactly on the principles which, presumably, Mr. Eliot would approve, since it is a tentative elucidation of a confused subject-matter which concludes neither in laws nor in judgments but only in one or two modest beams of light. None the less, " The Craft of Fiction " is one of the best books of general criticism which have been written of late years in English. It would be impossible here to do justice either to the grace of its style or to the penetration with which it examines the problem set forth : I can only make use of it for the light which it throws upon the possibilities and limitations of the scientific approach in criticism.

Mr. Lubbock starts by enlarging on the general, but often forgotten, truth that it is only with great difficulty and in disconnected flashes that even an intelligent reader gains any idea of the real " form," or shape, of a book, since the shape of a book is evolved in time, not in space, and cannot be present to a consciousness as an instantaneous whole. He sees that the proper reading of a book requires, therefore, a creative effort on the reader's part, and observes that the reader who has a general knowledge of literary materials, processes and possibilities will be best equipped to make this effort. And what afflicts Mr. Lubbock, as he tries to put the reader of novels in possession of this precious knowledge, is that during the century and a half over which the novel has flourished, criticism has arrived at no nomenclature, no recognisable commonplaces, no critical vocabulary which would make the discussion of novelistic processes easy, as the discussion of dramatic poetry was easy for Dryden and Johnson. Those who would cry out " Pedantry ! " at this would be singularly beside the mark, for Mr. Lubbock's approach to the novel is the same as Aristotle's approach to the drama in the *Poetics*. He wants to know, and to inquire into, the nature of the art of writing novels by examining the best instances and the greatest works of art in the kind. When an inquirer with such an end in view, finds common language hazy and inadequate he has a certain right to complain.

However, those who read Mr. Lubbock's book without prejudice will not find any inventions of critical jargon issuing from his very modest inquiry. Premising that in the ideal work of art form and matter coincide—" the book in which the matter is all used up in the form, in which the form expresses all the matter "—he proceeds to conduct an impressive and exceedingly interesting analysis of some of the world's greatest novels, Tolstoy's " War and Peace " and " Anna Karenina," Flaubert's " Madame Bovary," Thackeray's " Vanity Fair " and " Esmond," Henry James's " The Ambassadors " and " The Wings of the Dove," Balzac's " Eugénie Grandet " and one or two others by the way. Many pages of admirable literary criticism are the fruit of this analysis, which aims at revealing the progressive complications in the technique of presenting a story that have been evolved in practice : I note, as particularly good reading, the disentanglement of the two threads in " War and Peace," the appreciation of Thackeray's broad pictorial

sweep in " Vanity Fair," the clear exposition
of Henry James's later method in " The
Ambassadors " the observations on the failures
in craft, each different in kind, which occur in
Tolstoy's novels and in Thackeray's, all Chapter
VIII with its enlightening discussion of the
pictorial and dramatic methods and the essay
upon the limitations to the device of the
personal narrator contained in Chapter IX.
Mr. Lubbock's pages are full of clear and true
observations on the art of fiction which one
reads with a pleasant but surprised recognition
of their truth. Thus, of the set scene in fiction :

" On the whole, no doubt, the possibilities
of the scene are greatly abused in fiction, in the
daily and familiar novel. They are doubly
abused ; for the treatment of the scene is
neglected, and yet it recurs again and again,
much too often, and its value is wasted. It has
to be remembered that drama is the novelist's
highest light, like the white paper or white
paint of a draughtsman ; to use it prodigally
where it is not needed is to lessen its force where
it is essential. And so the economical procedure
would be to hoard it rather, reserving it for
important occasions—as in Bovary, sure
enough."

In England, at all events, nobody seems to have taken the trouble to point out this kind of truth before; and nobody certainly has attempted anything like this orderly examination of the gradual tendency of the artist in fiction to intensify, by refinements of dramatic technique, the primitive saga-form of narration. The possibilities of development, Mr. Lubbock thinks, reached their culmination in Henry James's method of objectifying an observing mind, at once mirror and object, as the medium of narration. In my opinion, this is not true. There were objections so strongly felt to Henry James's later method—the most fundamental one being that his objectification was a false one, since it was really a projection of his own unmistakable personality into one of the characters—that novelists recently have refused to learn from it anything at all; whereas all kinds of other experiments in the disintegration of strict narrative have lately been made by Miss Dorothy Richardson, Mrs. Woolf, Miss Stella Benson and above all by Mr. James Joyce. But this is by the way : it would lead us too far to amplify the matter here. The point to be made is that Mr. Lubbock, whether or no he is always correct in his judgments, has conducted in this book a legitimate scientific inquiry into a recognisable literary subject-matter : and the opinion at which he arrives is that only by far more extensive and painstaking inquiries of a similar nature could the criticism of fiction be reduced to anything like order and coherence. I give two extracts from his concluding chapter :

"I can imagine that by examining and comparing in detail the workmanship of many novels by many hands a critic might arrive at a number of inductions in regard to the relative properties of the scene, the incident dramatized, the incident pictured, the panoramic impression and the rest ; there is scope for a large inquiry, the results of which are greatly needed by a critic of fiction, not to speak of the writers of it. The few books that I have tried to take to pieces and to reconstruct are not enough—or at least it would be necessary to deal with them more searchingly."

"The business of criticism in the matter of fiction seems clear, at any rate. There is nothing more that can be usefully said about a novel until we have fastened upon the question of its making and explored it to some purpose. In all our talk about novels we are

hampered and held up by our unfamiliarity with
what is called their technical aspect, and that
is consequently the aspect to confront. That
Jane Austen was an acute observer, that
Dickens was a great humorist, that George
Eliot had a deep knowledge of provincial
character, that our living romancers are so full
of life that they are neither to hold nor to
bind—we know, we have repeated, we have told
each other a thousand times ; it is no wonder
that attention flags when we hear it all again.
It is their books, as well as their talents and
attainments, that we aspire to see—their books,
which we must recreate for ourselves if we are
ever to behold them. And in order to recreate
them durably there is the one obvious way—to
study the craft, to follow the process, to read
constructively. The practice of this method
appears to me at this time of day, I confess, the
only interest of the criticism of fiction."

It is at this point, with all our admiration for
Mr. Lubbock's work, that we begin to formulate
our misgivings : we suspect that he is exag-
gerating, that he is pressing his point of view
unduly, and we seem to catch sight of the
limitations to the scientific approach in
criticism. Even at first sight, there is some-

thing distinctly repellent in the idea of this extensive laboratory work. The prospect of a thousand earnest researchers in literary laboratories, armed with foot-rules and callipers, classifying " processes," docketing " pictorial " and " scenic " approaches, and tabulating shades in the relations between subject-matter and narrative medium is one at which the imagination boggles, in the justifiable conviction that in nine cases out of ten the classification would be entirely valueless. Do we not know, after all, the kind of book which graduates and professors of lesser American universities are apt to produce—self-styled analyses of the short story or the novel complete with curves and diagrams, all jargon and joinery, useless to practitioners and misleading to students ? The scientific spirit misapplied leads to these cold nullities, which need to be warmed and materialised to useful ashes on a bonfire. Mr. Lubbock's book is good and stimulating, but why ? Because he tacitly abandons the narrowness of his method and " abounds," as his master would have said, in that ampler consideration of artistic beauty and form as a whole which can be applied to novels with no more difficulty than it has for centuries been applied to poetry. " I am not trying, of course, to criticise ' Vanity Fair,' " says Mr. Lubbock at one place ; at another he says the same about " Anna Karenina." He implies by this that these inquiries of his are not criticism, as they would certainly not be in the majority of hands. But what gives them value in his hands is that they *become* criticism, and very good criticism ; so good, that one overlooks an instance or two of those inevitable infelicities to which technical criticism of art is apt to lead, such as the invitation to imagine how Balzac would have written " Anna Karenina."

It is to be remarked, moreover, that when Mr. Lubbock is well-settled in his stride, analysing or appreciating a book which he loves, he does not appear to find any difficulty in expressing his delicate perceptions with perfect precision in plain, intelligible language. He proves, in fact, that studying the craft, following the process, and reading constructively are all very well, if taste, feeling and intellectual insight are already there : but if they are wanting, what a plaiting of straw may not this vaunted process be ! Even in Mr. Lubbock's own performance there is, now and then, a challenge to the adequacy of his view of the critical problem. For instance,

it appears from his elucidation of the craft of
fiction that, in spite of his unbounded admiration for Tolstoy's artistic greatness, he must find
great leakages and deficiencies of craftsmanship
both in " War and Peace " and in " Anna
Karenina " : in " Madame Bovary," on the
other hand, he can find none, apparently
considering it perfect as an example of a certain
method. As a critical position this is obviously
partial and inconclusive, and Mr. Lubbock's
own book proves it to be so, since his pages on
Tolstoy's novels, for intellectual grasp of beauty
and sheer intellectual adequacy, are far superior
to those on " Madame Bovary." The two
great novels of genius, in fact, wherein craftsmanship so demonstrably failed, live again with
undiminished splendour in the enthusiasm of
this craftsman, whose admiration for the
faultless craft of Flaubert yet presents his
work to us cold and lifeless. How differently,
for instance, " Madame Bovary " appears,
how brilliant and vital, in that very essay by
Mr. Middleton Murry wherein Flaubert's
failings are relentlessly exposed ! Examine
craftsmanship as he may, in fine, when
Mr. Lubbock judges he judges with all his
intelligence, and he cannot help judging when
he believes himself to be only taking to pieces.

The process gives him his standpoint, it is true ; but the crystallisation, the fusion, of thought and feeling are what give him his value as a critic.

And we come thus back to the truth that good criticism is as little a formula of craftsmanship as of ethics or science. It is the work of all good critics who, each in his individual way, apply thought and feeling to the objectification of a work of art. An Aristotle goes to work in one manner, a Coleridge in another ; and by the barest and most meagre of hypotheses the genius of the one will reach unapproachable heights, while the most transcendental gyrations on the verge of the inane will suddenly land the other on a pinnacle of solid truth. Between these extremes there are infinite gradations of critical equipment and achievement : but at all times it is the mind of the critic that matters more than his view of the correct critical procedure.

VI

PRACTICAL CRITICS.

THE impulse to practical criticism is not so much a predisposition as the conclusion of a utilitarian argument. Creative, or self-expressive, criticism and scientific, or inquisitory, criticism are symptoms of fundamental attitudes to life and to art. All men and women share these conflicting symptoms in infinitely varying degrees : one or other is usually predominant, and when, by a rare combination of psychological elements, a critic of permanent value appears, his work shows on which side the predominance lies, whether he holds it more important to proclaim the conviction that is urgent or to search for the truth that is hidden. Even here, of course, there is always the practical element, the will resulting in action and the useful end in view : but when a critic is observed to be turning his back on practical considerations, neglecting his audience, for instance, fatiguing them, despising them, caring little whether he pleases or whether his subject is popular, then it may be presumed that this element is an unimportant one on his critical activity. On the other hand, for the majority of practising critics, in whose minds the balance of the two fundamental predispositions is fluctuating, the practical element is decisive. Their work is done because, for a variety of practical reasons, it has to be done, and in a certain way and in a certain form because that way and that form are useful. In fact, to use an analogy from English political life, as the Labour Party represents certain concrete economic facts, ways of life and material aspirations, while Liberalism and Conservatism are, in their essentials, attitudes of mind, so practical criticism stands alongside of, yet not wholly uniform with, the creative and the scientific. Moreover, as the Labour Party, by its very constitution, is less purely political than the other two, so practical criticism is less purely critical. But this does not in the least mean that it is less valuable or, of necessity, less beautiful. One can imagine how a critic with something of the self-expressive energy possessed by Mr. D. H. Lawrence would handle the work of Tolstoy : he would throw all he knew of it, and much else, into the crucible of his imagination and, before the reader's eyes, fuse either a part of himself into the image of Tolstoy, or a part of Tolstoy into the image of himself. The scientific critic, on the other hand, would deal with Tolstoy after the manner of Mr. Lubbock, his interest being in using Tolstoy's work to prove something about literary art altogether outside this particular instance : and he might write, as Mr. Lubbock writes in " The Craft of Fiction " :

" In War and Peace, as it seems to me, the story suffers twice over for the imperfection of the form. It is damaged, in the first place, by the importation of another and an irrelevant story—damaged because it so loses the sharp and clear relief that it would have if it stood alone. Whether the story was to be the drama of youth and age, or the drama of war and peace, in either case it would have been incomparably more impressive if all the great wealth of the material had been used for its purpose, all brought into one design. And furthermore, in either case again, the story is incomplete ; neither of them is finished, neither of them is given its full development, for all the size of the book . . . . Tolstoy's novel is wasteful of its subject ; that is the whole objection to its loose, unstructural form. Criticism bases its conclusion upon nothing whatever but the injury done to the story, the loss of its full potential value."

Neither of these methods is typical of the practical critic, whose mental temperature is rarely at the fusing point, while his aim is less to establish general conclusions by picking works of art to bits, than to give a reasonable estimate of a particular work or works of art. The immediate aims of practical criticism are many—instruction, entertainment, the divulgation of the new, the reassessment of the old, the foundation of public taste, the satisfaction of public curiosity. The practical critic serves the public as taster, as judge and as pedagogue, preserving its conservative prejudices from too revolutionary attacks while assisting in their gradual transformation. He may be professor, historian, lecturer, writer of books, or journalist ; and the excellences to which he may attain are not uniform. One may excel as a writer of prose, another as a purveyor of knowledge ; one as trustworthy guide to the past, another as a sympathetic interpreter of to-day ; one as a preserver of

169

tradition, another as a destroyer of complacency. A critic who has served his generation faithfully in any of these ways, whether his written word perish with him or no, has justified his existence and earned a right to praise. Those who live too high in the realm of pure ideas, as well as those who keep their eyes too low upon the manifestations of that highly commercialised product, the modern newspaper, are easily tempted to think with scorn of English criticism, on the one hand because it is not analytic and, on the other, because at its lowest it is purely narrative and mechanical. Such a view is unjust. Practical criticism, taken as a whole, is very good in England, and at any given moment, the number of useful, honest and capable critics is remarkable. Dr. Johnson was a man of unusual powers, it is true, but it is not unreasonable to regard his " Lives of the Poets " as a type of practical criticism in English. They were undertaken as a task, for a bookseller's edition of the poets : and, though their critical standpoint has been superseded, they live yet for their liveliness, their graceful style and their good sense. Johnson's ease of expression and his compelling manner are not for everyone, especially in these days of

self-questioning and nervous instability ; but
one need only spend an hour with a library
catalogue to realise what quantities of excellent
work in this line alone have been produced.
No country in Europe has anything better
to show, in its kind, than the " English Men
of Letters " series : and the amount of good
work that has been put into introductions,
summaries and critico-biographical monographs by English critics is enormous.
The English critic, like the English civil
servant, puts up with obscurity. More than
half the best book reviewing is anonymous,
and it is unquestionable that brilliant introductions written for popular reprints, of which
instances abound, bring their author no
adequate reward either in fame or payment.
A critic knows this beforehand, yet he does the
work with the help of that strange regulator
known as the British conscience, which forces
upon him a sense of responsibility in detail,
a disinterested expenditure of time and labour
and a pride in the professional efficiency
with which his task is carried out. It is the
same with the reviewing of books in this
country, which, if not always " serious " in
Mr. Eliot's esoteric sense, is distinguished
on all but the low levels, by a measure of dignity,

good sense, diligence and grace of expression, qualities which have earned for it respect, if they have earned little else.

The most noticeable failings of practical English criticism are incompleteness, rhetoric and insularity, all of which commend themselves to the English mind in general so that they pass unnoticed. Partly owing to purely material considerations of space and time, partly owing to the national desultoriness of mind, it is characteristic of English criticism to leap from one critical topic to another with considerable agility, but to lose the plastic effect of the whole performance by failing to round off one movement before another is begun. Rhetoric, which we use so feebly in our public speaking, is the darling vice of all our prose. Only our strongest writers can avoid the temptation, when the itch is in their fingers, to let appeals to facile emotion take the place of careful argument and to conceal an untidy thought in a gaudy outer garment of words. As for insularity, it is a part of our intellectual and moral integument, which is so familiar to us as to be unnoticeable. Insularity is not the same as self-centredness. The French are intensely self-centred, judging all forms of expression

from the standpoint of their own mentality,
but to ideas themselves they erect no barrier,
secure in their capability of accommodating
any idea without effort and without exaggera-
tion : but we English set up a customs barrier
to ideas themselves, and when they have paid
their footing we accommodate them, painfully
at first and then, sometimes, with hysterical
effusiveness which only proves our insular
awkwardness, we perform antics of salutation
to them which are little else than comic.
The English volume of fragmentary homages
to Marcel Proust was a case in point. Could
anything have been more unnecessary or
ridiculous than this uncertain chorus of
miscellaneous voices in honour of a remarkable
and recently dead French novelist ? That
the French themselves should produce a funeral
wreath of literary flowers was natural and
intelligible : it is a Latin custom to pronounce
orations over the tombs of the departed. But
it is not a Latin custom to pronounce orations
over departed foreign artists whose tombs are
in their native country : and it would certainly
not be expected that, on the death of some
British writer equal in calibre to M. Proust—
and I am bold enough to assert confidently
that such exist—a curious collection of French

novelists and men of letters, should record in
a volume a very mixed and imperfect comprehension of the art to which their tribute was
dedicated. Having a supreme sense of dignity
and fitness, French men of letters would
instinctively avoid putting themselves in so
false a position, in which they could neither
confer honour nor receive gratitude : the
aptitude for blundering publicly with good
intent is a peculiar gift of the Teutonic strain
which we must accept with resignation.
Englishmen, indeed, have an incorrigible tendency to make themselves ridiculous when they
approach a foreign literature, be it with suspicion, defiance or enthusiasm. I read lately
a page in a weekly journal in which a still
sucking critic expressed his view that, since the
death of Marcel Proust, Pirandello was the
greatest living writer. This view was
apparently based upon a reading in English
translation of three plays, two of which were,
indeed, the most brilliant performances of
this ingenious and prolific writer : but the
utterer of this sweeping judgment showed no
sign of having studied the works of this author
in the original, or of knowing how they are
related to Italian literature as a whole, or how
regarded by those who are best competent

to speak for Italian tradition. Not to mention that he made no attempt to justify his exaltation of Pirandello above all the living writers in all the nations. That is the kind of performance which insularity induces and which makes the explanation of English criticism to intelligent men of other European nations sometimes so bewildering a business. Our levity, at times, appears to be nothing less than monstrous.

Insularity, indeed, is a permanent condition of nearly all our criticism. Even sound and truly valuable critics are afflicted by it, nor are they therefore so desperately to blame. Historically and geographically, this little island is severed from the rest of Europe, and it is useless to pretend that this is not so, or to repine when one finds, in conversation with intelligent Europeans, that we are undeniably cut off from the current of general European culture that seems to circulate throughout the continent. It is the eddies and back washes of these currents which reach us, at times propelled with an accidental force which produces surprisingly sudden erosions of opinion. Though it is possible to be sufficiently detached to observe this, it is unreasonable not to accept it. An Englishman finds exceeding

difficulty in combating the instinct to judge
the literature of his own country by, broadly
speaking, parochial standards, on a kind of
tacit assumption that the bulk of contemporary
Europe writes nothing worth considering at
all. It is only to be expected that this attitude
should extend itself to our criticism of foreign
literature which, though individual writers
and works of art are often acutely discussed
in isolation, is seldom considered as a part of
a great development. Here is the gravamen
of Mr. T. S. Eliot's charge, though he puts
it in a manner which repels by its curtness.
That we so seldom take art " seriously " is
only a symptom of insularity. We ought to be
more conscious than we are of *all* literature
as a developed whole ; and, as critics, we
ought to know and study more, or else have
the grace to speak only, and the perseverance
to speak fully, of what we do know and have
studied. Of knowledge and study, at all
events, as effective specifics against instinctive
British tendencies, Professor Saintsbury has
set an admirable example. Nobody could
entirely acquit him of insularity : he, too,
obviously glories in the predilections of a
vigorous personal temperament and affects
that particular form of insularity which is

displayed in Oxford Common rooms and which has so afflicted his prose style with the strange allusive humours of its conversation, as to render it at times almost incomprehensible to the uninitiated. But these are superficial blemishes in comparison to the virtue of his thoroughness. He has boasted, with justification, that he has never judged at second hand, and any reader who profits by his work may be certain that, whether his subject is English or foreign literature, every text, no matter how unimportant, and every other criticism, no matter how insignificant, will have been sifted in his capacious intellectual machinery. His delightful and exhaustive " History of the French Novel," with all its refusal to push personal taste aside in the final arbitration, is a proof that enthusiasm and understanding can refine insularity from an obvious limitation to an amiable and even picturesque quality.

I cannot, however, forbear to illustrate the insidious nature of English critical weaknesses from the works of another critic of repute whose embodiment of English critical virtues nobody could wish to deny. Mr. John Bailey's taste is that of the cultivated English gentleman at its highest, based as it is on a true appreciation of the great poets and writers of Greece and Rome, enriched by long acquaintance with the serene, unquestioned masters of literature in other ages, and informed by the sane, yet liberal, conception of life and human character which is, or certainly has been in the past, a British quality worthy of admiration by others and of pride in ourselves. When Mr. Bailey writes of what he loves and reveres, he unfailingly combines delight with instruction. Few more charming books for instance, have appeared in our day than his " Dr. Johnson and his Circle," and in no book is there to be found a juster critical appreciation of Johnson's place, both as man and writer. A reader might be sure that, whenever he saw Mr. Bailey's name at the head of an essay on one of the great worthies of English literature, he would be stimulated and entertained by what followed. But where this mellow taste is not involved and when controversy is the topic, Mr. Bailey is not so impeccable. The English weaknesses intrude. We may find them in his latest book of critical essays : " The Continuity of Letters." There appears in this book a discussion of modern poetry, which is sensible in the main but extremely

incomplete in its survey. Mr. Bailey contrasts
a good short poem by Mr. Walter de la Mare
with an ejaculatory, rather uncouth one by
Mr. Robert Graves ; the name of Mr. Graves
suggests the bare mention of Mr. W. H. Davies ;
the tendency of modern poets in general, to
indulge in descriptive journalism is then
chastised, an inadequate, though not unjust,
page is given to George Meredith's poetry,
and then Mr. Bailey diverts the current of
discussion to Gray, with whom he is once more
at home.

This is a typically English example of
critical incompleteness : and there is another
example of it combined with an unnecessarily
rhetorical appeal. On the subject of " Poetry
and Commonplace " Mr. Bailey indignantly
exclaims against the remark of some unnamed
person that Gray's " Elegy " was " the
quintessence of commonplace." He begins
his defence with a fine and eloquent analysis
of the first stanza, pointing out how rich the
sound, how simple the imagery, and how
suitable the expression : but here he
unfortunately abandons analysis for a rhetorical
apostrophe beginning, " What a stanza ! "
and ending : " A quintessence of commonplace indeed ! Would we had another like

it in the language ! " All this is very creditable
to his sentiments, but it does not really meet
the real critical case of Gray's " Elegy," which
is to decide whether as a whole, it is one of the
absolutely great and perfect poems, or whether
its perfect parts are not joined together with
patterns of ample, shapely rhetoric which are
poetry of the second class, decorative, emotional
perhaps, but not profoundly significant.
Ejaculations addressed to an imaginary audience
of anthology-readers will not settle a question
of this kind : for the question is serious, and
ejaculations are not.

As for insularity, I have already noted in
an earlier chapter Mr. Lytton Strachey's
admirable correction of Mr. Bailey's insular
view of Racine. There is a strange paragraph
in " The Continuity of Letters " about
Dostoievsky, occurring in the chapter upon
Don Quixote to which all lovers of the doleful
knight will heartily subscribe. Quite reasonably, Mr. Bailey complains at the outset that
Dostoievsky only gives us the extremes—the
divine and the bestial—in human life, and very
little of harmony between body, mind and
soul, of happiness, of good sense and of good
conduct. We want, he says, more of the
golden middle, and in reaction against this

fierceness, we turn to Molière, Dickens or the serenity of Gibbon's Autobiography. This, of course, is but the expression of a particular mental reaction, perfectly legitimate, though not criticism. But the last few sentences go beyond the line of the legitimate :

" Only with the true classics emotion has nothing to do. It is extravagance, eccentricity, violence, that the classics avoid. The note of the classic is centrality and sanity. Homer, Sophocles, Horace, Shakespeare, Cervantes, Molière, Scott : none of these were cranky men. If the Slav wishes to be of their company he must learn to add some geniality and common sense to his heights and depths, to be healthier and more catholic in his savour of life."

Now, presuming that by " a classic," Mr. Bailey means a literary work of supreme artistic excellence, this is a strange artistic criterion, which seems to be partly social, partly athletic and wholly British. But it is the hectoring " John Bullishness " of the last patronising recommendation to " the Slav " that arouses our concern. It is an uncalled-for self-exposure on a critic's part, all the more distressing in that one can imagine a devastating retort on the Slav's part, in which he might comment pungently on Mr. Bailey's conception of Shakespeare, and express complete equanimity at exclusion from the society of Horace and Scott, if he might share that of Aeschylus, Dante and Tolstoy. This is not to dispute that a competent criticism of Dostoievsky might not be developed from the principles of classicism, for it certainly could : but this impotent and rhetorical lecturing of another nation's artists in general is a gratuitous exhibition of a common British tendency at which, I confess, I blush uncomfortably. Younger critics, at all events, will not go far wrong if they add to their daily meditations this : that even a lifelong study of a foreign nation's literature in all its historical, intellectual and social conditions will rarely place a critic in the position to say one word of real value or originality to the cultivated minds of that particular nation, much less to offer it advice. To free his own nationals from ignorance and prejudice will be task enough for him, if to exhort, rather than to expound, is the purpose that he follows.

It is undoubtedly safer for the practical critic to expound, yet even in so doing it is

hard for him, if he be English, to escape
insularity. Contemporary criticism, therefore,
has no surer ground for gratitude to Dr.
Edmund Gosse that he has shown with
what grace and ease insularity may be avoided
while nationality is preserved. Nobody could
call his work insular, yet how admirably English
it is, throughout, from his masterpiece of art
" Father and Son " to the slightest of his
urbane reflections upon a book of the day !
And it is not knowledge alone which preserves
him from that failing in critical virtue—for
knowledge has never been a secure buckle
against temperament—but it is his detachment
from unessentials and his firm grasp of essentials.
Reading again, in the volume "Aspects and
Impressions," his admirable study of two
French critics, Emile Faguet and Remy de
Gourmont, one has a grateful sense of the
delicate illumination that ensues when a fine
and sympathetic understanding is turned upon
any corner of the artistic field. Dr. Gosse
is not, perhaps, purely or principally, a critic :
he is a literary historian, a biographer, an
essayist, a conversationalist, but all his gifts
may be combined in the title which has a
prouder sound in French than in English,
homme de lettres. Between him and a

Brunetière, a Lemaître, a Faguet, a
Gourmont, or a Gide, there are profound
differences, and yet one could proceed from
consideration of his work to that of a notable
French critic without any readjustment of
focus : there would be no break in the
continuity, and no lapse in the tradition.
There is the same finished handling of tools,
the same clarity of vision, the same certainty
of direction. If there were a contest in
criticism at some ideal and intellectual
Olympiad, no other than this veteran of
English letters could fitly captain the English
team, for with his suppleness and polish and
understanding he could temper the crudity
of his subalterns while yielding little to their
youth in pungency of word or precision of
attack.

Here is a veteran who is also a contemporary :
still, as the swordsmen say, " il a des jambes."
It would be difficult to forget his signal proof
of this in the first number of the *London
Mercury*. There was youth striking out a
new line with admirable daring in none too
prosperous a field. The leader was young
and so were most of the squadron gathered
under the orange banner : but in the first
day's skirmish, at all events, an older knight

lent them his wit, and to the spectator nothing was more impressive than the old knight's prowess. Dr. Gosse's contribution to that first number was the paper on George Eliot, which heads the volume "Aspects and Impressions." I doubt if he has ever written a more finished piece of critical presentation, from its typical opening paragraph containing a sharply-outlined satirical impression of George Lewes and his lady driving in a victoria, to the final just appraisement of her once unduly revered genius. With its smoothness of direction, its ease of motion, the astringent humour which braced its periods, and the rich beam of personal knowledge which it cast upon a bygone generation, it was a work of art from which a younger writer, if wise, would have ruefully admitted that he had plenty to learn. And, so long as Dr. Gosse continues the weekly exhibition of a master's craft, the happy opportunity of learning will remain—of learning, that is, lightness of approach, agility in the use of wide knowledge, neatness and urbanity in delivering a point, co-ordination of movement, quickness in covering the ground, and, above all, that incisiveness in drawing a feature or describing a character, in which, undoubtedly, Dr. Gosse displays an inimitable felicity. One need only look through any volume of "Books on the Table" to see the happy interplay of these qualities from which, though Dr. Gosse has never desired to be a prophet and is not inspired to elucidate beyond a certain point, instruction and enjoyment are inevitably mingled in the reader's mind. And if Croce's view is correct that criticism is "the serene narration of what has happened," so charming a narration of literary facts and so brilliant a delineator of literary personalities as the author of "The Life of Algernon Charles Swinburne" is assured of a higher place in the critical pantheon than, in his modesty, he might claim for himself. Moreover, throughout the wide range of his comment upon literature, it is to be observed that a distinctly remarkable absence of solemnity has been accompanied by an equally remarkable presence of seriousness. It would have been impossible, indeed, to attain such skill without it.

From Dr. Edmund Gosse, by way of the already mentioned *London Mercury*, one modulates inevitably to the name of Mr. J. C. Squire, poet, essayist, critic and editor : and the modulation is made all the more inevitable

by the fact that on most Sundays in the week
the cultivated minds who are not entertained
after breakfast by Dr. Gosse's dexterity find
solace in Mr. Squire's wise mixture of humour
and good sense. To enjoy both is a counsel
of perfection with which many people find it
easy to comply. That Mr. Squire, in his
early middle years, has become one of our
leading men of letters is due to qualities wholly
different from those of Dr. Gosse. He is not
urbane, polished, detached, delicately pungent ;
he cannot draw incisive vignettes, and the gait
of his prose, though sturdy and sometimes
stately, is a little cumbrous ; and he is certainly
not in the main continental tradition, but one
might rather say that he was avowedly and
intentionally remaining an Englishman, like
the brave mariner in Gilbert's " Pinafore,"
in order to carry out his appointed work, the
enlightenment of an insular audience. As a
critic and a commentator upon letters, as a
writer and also as an editor, he has a profound
sense of practical purpose, and it is here, in a
chapter on a practical criticism, that emphasis
needs to be laid. Always, whether in the garb
of that humorous sage called Solomon Eagle,
as founder and editor of a successful literary
review or as introducer of the " book of the

week " to a Sunday audience, he has not scrupled to betray his wholesome conviction that a man of letters should adapt himself to his environment and speak so as to be understood by far more than one layer of the reading public. He has said in one of his shorter critiques that the literature which obtains and keeps a hold on people does not make its principal appeal to the recognising eye or even to the understanding, but, as he implies, to the broad common consciousness of average humanity. He is almost unfairly contemptuous at moments, of cleverness, sheer intellect, exquisite treatment, and all manifestations of art which presuppose a high degree of intelligence for their appreciation, though his attitude is not continuous and is tempered by the undoubted appreciations of his own intelligence such as inspired him to write his review of M. de la Mare's " The Midget," or his notes on the lyric poetry of Dr. Bridges. He is unblushing in his respect for common, not esoteric, morality, he insists that the verdict of a man's peers at large has importance, and he is inclined, when a creative writer seems to have ignored his maxim that " poetry is an expression of gratitude for things enjoyed," to sum up his excellences a little grudgingly, as in the typical conclusion to his essay on Baudelaire (in " Books Reviewed ").

" He wrote impeccable prose ; but his verse, for compactness, for accuracy, for music, cannot be surpassed. He may not be ranked with the world's greatest poets : humanity will scarcely conceive that to a man whose principal work was labelled (not without reason) ' Flowers of Evil,' and who was successfully prosecuted for obscenity : apart from which, volume of work and universality of appeal are bound to count in such matters. But there certainly never was a poet who said with more perfection what he had to say, who had fewer weak lines or otiose words, who was more consistently near his own highest level of achievement. His sense of form was like that of the great masters in marble and bronze, and he worked like a slave in his narrow field, watering it with his sweat ' pour extorquer quelques épis. . . . .' To read him is to contract disgust with looseness and diffuseness. It is perhaps significant that the memorial ode which the young Swinburne wrote on him was the most clear, vivid, and truly classic of all Swinburne's poems."

Well, there was more to be said than that :

189

and one recognises that Baudelaire was not
in the direct line of Mr. Squire's critical leanings.
Yet, in the main, it was not unjust, and its
deficiencies border the very virtues which have
enabled Mr. Squire to serve his generation
so admirably. It has been his aim as a critic
to light and keep burning a lamp of sound
and cultivated opinion which shall throw an
even ray over the past and the present of literature, as men in their passage through the
confused market-place of life shall catch a
glimpse of them. He sees the critic neither
as the preacher nor as the judge, but as the
lantern-bearer privileged above all to illuminate
the new treasures of truth and beauty and
laughter which contemporary poets and prose-
writers are giving to the world : and the
peculiar charm and mellowness of his beam
is due less to any formal aesthetic merit than
to the subtle essence of the personality which
feeds the beacon-flame. To see other critics
who, in a spiritual exaltation, overlook plain
beauty of sound and gracefulness of image or
who, in an excess of scientific near-sightedness,
seem to lose the larger and kindlier prospects
of literature, makes him impatient, for, being
a poet himself, he will not admit that an
exquisite sense of quality need render a critic's

palate as exclusive as a tea-taster's. As a prose-writer he is not a great stylist. He will write hastily at times, though never obscurely, and the pleasant flavour of his essays is often accompanied by a certain roughness : but his maturest prose has a quality which gives it a clearly distinguishable character. This quality twinkles in his quiet parentheses, such as the final sentence of his chapter on Mr. A. E. Housman's poems, " Even hymn-writers could study him to advantage " ; it shines steadily in many pages of his longer essays and in such shorter reviews as that of " Back to Methusaleh " and of Croce's essay on Shakespeare ; and it becomes radiant in such a passage as that* in which he reflects on the great and solemn subjects which have brought a " large utterance " to the lips of English writers.

" Time, Death, Eternity, Mutability : those words, the most awful that we know, insistently recur . . . . Those names, those figures with their skirts of thunder and doom, trail through all our literature with a majesty that no others possess. Apostrophising these, our shadowy tyrants, celebrating them, rebelling against

* " Essays in Poetry." *Prose and Morality.*

them, we may clothe our conceptions in many images . . . . But those shapes tower over our whole world. Anything we look at in the sunlight, a wave, a weed, a travelling insect, may be like a window opening out to them ; and at night, under the dark sky, so actual and so symbolical, the reflective man is always aware of them. We have our activities and our distractions. We must satisfy our carnal cravings, eat, drink and sleep . . . . But whenever the moment comes that we turn round from our toys it is one spectacle that we see : life proceeding from darkness to darkness, change, dissolution and death. And the greatest utterance of our tongue is a chronicle, again and again resumed and repeated, of the wonder and dread, the certain regret and the wavering hope which that spectacle arouses in hearts which have immortal longings but have loved transient things . . . ."

My space is too short to contain the whole passage, in which the poet's music proves the critic's judgment : but it leads me to suggest that the quality of Mr. Squire's critical prose springs from his vision of human life. Man and the works of man, very beautiful, exquisitely foolish, as real but as transitory as

a beam of light, his immortal longings, his
transient loves—it is the spectacle of these that
in mid-task catches his eye and inspires him to
praise what is good, if only in intention, to
laugh kindly at folly, to help, even a little,
and play a man's part *before it is too late*. The
deep northern wistfulness, unattainable by
Latins and barely intelligible to them, vibrates
through his prose as well as through his verse ;
but its *timbre* is thoroughly English, like that
of the clarinet, producing a melody that is
equable and sane, yet with possibilities of a
sudden depth and richness which are all the
more effective for the economy of their use.
Mr. Squire has had his disputes with his
contemporaries, or has been the cause of them.
His conception of poetry and his dislike both of
excessive idealism and exaggerated formalities
have roused protest, but never bitterness ;
for there has at no time been any doubt of his
wholehearted devotion to the craft and the
tradition of English letters. By a combination
of creative powers and gifts of organisation,
by his own practice and by the encouragement
of others he has been able to serve his literary
generation more signally than most men of
his years. As a critic, he has judged art
sanely because he understands the ever-

widening circles to which it appeals. " To
a thousand cavils one answer is sufficient ;
the purpose of a writer is to be read, and the
criticism which would destroy the power
of pleasing, must be blown aside." These
words of Dr. Johnson,* one might guess, have
been the inspiration of Mr. Squire's criticism,
for he, like Johnson and unlike many critics,
has ever been deeply conscious of a deep and
real affinity with his human brothers. Other
art may be exclusive, other criticism trenchant or
ironic ; but where art is genuine and criticism
truly sensitive, the warmth and vigour
added to them by broad human sympathy
can hardly be over-estimated.

There can be diversity, however, even in
broad human sympathy, as might be shown,
did not the modest scope of this book forbid
it, by a detailed comparison of Mr. Robert
Lynd's critical work with that of Mr. Squire.
The literary editor of the *Daily News* holds a
position as practical critic analogous to that
of the editor of the *London Mercury* and chief
literary *conferencier* of the *Observer*. Many
volumes attest his power of giving a brightness
and a permanent interest to the reviewing
of new books which is the occasion, skilfully

* Lives of the Poets : *Pope.*

though he often conceals it, of his critical action in general. Had I been dealing with the essay, that delicate and inimitable flower of English literature, Mr. Lynd's ripe art, which plays humorously yet seldom trivially round the common phases of human life, would have been a leading theme. It is well-known with what grace of design, what felicity of expression and what ingenuity of varied cadence the middle article of the *New Statesman* delights its readers. Mr. Lynd is happiest when the roving of his fancy is not circumscribed, yet he brings the qualities of a finished essayist also into his criticism. Periodical reviews do not, as a rule, bear collection into volumes, but one who takes up Mr. Lynd's "Books and Authors" or "The Art of Letters" —to mention two of the more recent—will find himself led onwards through a remarkable diversity of subjects, familiar and unfamiliar, with a never-failing charm and a seldom-failing justice.

On the practice of criticism in general, Mr. Lynd professes sound views which he has developed in more than one essay. He holds that it is the critic's proudest function to praise, and that only what is bad in its kind should be condemned; he would rather scold a good artist for falling below his highest level than a popular entertainer for aiming surely at a modest mark; and he openly confesses that his notion of criticism comes near to portrait painting, thus artfully excusing his practice of rather neglecting a new book in hand in order to re-treat its subject with a deft brush.

These thumb-nail sketches of Mr. Lynd's, neat, fluent and often brilliant as they are, also derive much of their quality from their broad humanity, though it is a different humanity from Mr. Squire's, less wistful, less poetic, one might even say more robust. For Mr. Lynd, being an Irishman, is not in the least sentimental and not particularly reverent, in those matters, at any rate, where an Englishman is inclined to be both. " Herrick was a gross and good-natured clergyman who had a double chin. He kept a pet pig, which drank beer out of a tankard . . . ." " Charles Lamb was a small flat-footed man whose eyes were of different colours and who stammered." " Mr. Max Beerbohm generally leaves us with the impression that he has written something perfect." " Mr. Conrad is nothing of a peacock." " Lord Rosebery's oratory is the port at a banquet. It is a little somnolent in its charm." These are a few of

his beginnings which one may well contrast
with the lachrymose bows and scrapings of
more typically English critics, in whose postures,
I should say, Mr. Lynd often takes the same
malicious pleasure as Horace Walpole took in
the Duke of Newcastle's. His broad humanity
appeals to perceptions of ordinary men, while
Mr. Squire appeals more to their emotions :
he presents his subjects in clear lights and
well-defined attitudes which make an
immediate impression on the attention and
the memory. His criticism is a view from a
personal angle : and if the complaint were
made that his perspective sometimes needs
correction or that he illuminates occasionally the
less important features of his sitter, he would,
I daresay, cheerfully admit its justice. For
him, critical infallibility is a chimera : as
he says : " Milton was right when he made
'all-judging Jove' the one supreme critic
of literature. Meanwhile, the standards of
sub-lunar critics are but guesses. The critic
who claims that they are more is simply a
dogmatist who climbs into a pulpit when he
should be going on a pilgrimage." As this
is the end of a paragraph, one need not inquire
too closely into its cogency. Some men are
best at pilgrimages, others in the pulpit : but

of Mr. Lynd it may be said that his guesses are illuminating and his pilgrimage strikes out an admirable route.

Here, albeit summarily, this chapter must come to a close, though other practical critics of virtue and understanding might have claimed a place in it. The staff of the *Manchester Guardian* alone contains several, including that trumpet-major of English prose, Mr. C. E. Montague, whose literary criticism, however, is only occasional; the brilliantly witty criticism of Miss Rebecca West and Mrs. Woolf, though also occasional, would have deserved more than a word, especially upon my own view that both of these ladies, in their diligently personal approach to criticism, have always been far less insular than male critics of the same power ; and critics like Mr. Edward Shanks—whose " First Essays in Literature " contains a remarkably good chapter on Goethe —and Mr. J. B. Priestley—whose robust common sense finds a very polished expression —must perforce be left making, as they are, a promising entry into the company of leading critics. The position of practical, disinterested, sane and elegant English criticism is being well-kept up—that is the point which it has been the aim of this chapter to support.

Seriousness may sometimes be wanting, but seriousness is not everything ; insularity is certainly present, but it is a permanent condition of matters English for which there are compensations ; and while it is to be regretted that the bustle and clatter of to-day tends to hinder study and disturb reflection, we may congratulate ourselves that in this English-speaking country, at any rate, a critic can still dress just opinion in a dignified eloquence or a graceful humour and yet appeal to the understanding of his countrymen.

VII

TASTE AND LIFE: A CRITICAL PROBLEM OF TO-DAY AND TO-MORROW.

To write of the future in the present is always a dubious proceeding, since our faculties of looking forward are still rudimentary. The only defence of a mildly Promethean attitude is that its result is, in reality, a valuable commentary on the present, for the prophecies of a period are an excellent clue to its state of mind. At the present moment, however, when the future of almost every human institution seems to rest upon incalculable issues, and the values of all things—except health and wealth, unanimously desired—are called in question, no very startling forecasts of the future of literary criticism suggest themselves. One may be certain that the activity will continue to flourish for a long time to come, at least until the Shavian millennium when art is but a toy for children. How should it cease, indeed, so long as through criticism human minds are impelled to reveal the truths they apprehend, the discoveries they have made or the ripe judgments at which they have arrived ? The three dispositions—creative, scientific and practical—will continue to fashion thought after their respective impulses ; and the changes, the novelties, will come, not so much from the transformation of criticism itself, as from that of social conditions and mental outlook. Though the old inspirations to artistic creation will persist—the deep human emotions which psychology may explain but cannot remove—new imaginative impulses and new forms of art will be born ; in the different countries of the world and within the wider polity of nations the insatiable human demand for entertainment and information will take new directions ; and from epoch to epoch, as in the past, the orientation of creative minds will be altered by the slow pressure of imperceptible forces. Along with all such developments criticism will march, changing inevitably with the education and interests of its day, yet still remaining fundamentally the same instrument that now prepares the soil for creation and essays to sort the fruit. So long as there is art there will be criticism, and, even though writing and printing should become obsolete, the poem or novel broadcast through the world will be followed by " Hullo everybody ! The critic speaking."

The professional critic, as Mr. Middleton Murry has remarked, is and always will be at the mercy of circumstances, for the periodical press, where alone there is a certain and continuous market for his wares, must follow the interest of the moment. Books as they appear, personalities as they arise and centenaries as they mature will have to be dealt with ; and that critic is fortunate who has a wide range of interests. Moreover, it is not only that the subject of criticism eludes his personal control, but there is also the public to be considered. In no age is the influence of such contemporary conditions as the general state of a nation's mind, the general level of taste, and the immediate organisation of literary demand and opportunity, likely to be negligible. Coleridge had, of all men, a wayward and desultory mind, yet even he attempted to conform to them. And there will always be what Dryden, writing of the drama, called the three publics—the small public of the truly intelligent and cultivated, the rather larger public of " warm young men " whose artistic enthusiasms are real but sometimes shallow or misdirected, and the largest public of all which only requires to be entertained. It is here, perhaps, that one touches the chief critical problem of the present day for which the future will find a solution. In Anglo-Saxon countries, at all events, the conflict between these publics has become, of recent years, both accentuated and transformed. Even in the last two decades the gulf between two ideals, which for short I call " taste " and " life," has perceptibly widened : and the transformation lies in this that, whereas aforetime " taste " has carried the day with no difficulty, " life " now pulls with equal vigour. The article in a recent number of the *London Mercury* entitled " Modern Taste "* was an amusing symptom of this fact, but there are many others. There is the prevalence of the term " highbrow," an Americanism which is now used as a reproach to any form of art which demands a moderate proportion of intellect for its appreciation ; there is the enormous multiplication of popular periodicals whose aim, quite openly confessed, is not to supply art but entertainment or mental distraction ; and, in a word, there is strongly articulated an acceptance of the view, genuinely held though often artificially encouraged for

* See above, pp. 59-61.

commercial purposes, that the bare details and vicissitudes of human life, strange incident and varied action, and the simple emotions derived from the spectacle of these, are more satisfying and worth attention than subtle delineation of character, successful expression of profound thought, originality of imagination, and the perfection, in general, of artistic construction.

The conflict, of course, is not new, for it existed at all periods of conscious art. It was known in the days of Aristophanes and of Horace; Shakespeare had observed what " tickled the ears of the groundlings "; and, in fact, it is only rarely in any age that the now acknowledged masterpieces have appealed immediately to the wide popular taste. If there were nothing more than this to be observed in our own day, there would be no need to enlarge upon so common a theme. But the dissidence has entered upon a new phase which vitally concerns the critic and, even to the detached observer, is remarkably interesting. While, in earlier days the acclamations of the multitude were *critically* ineffectual against the verdict of the more cultivated and discriminating few, to-day the judgment of the great public has become so powerfully articulate that it has ranged genuine artists and critics on its side : it has added reason and intelligence to numbers, so that opposition, besides being unprofitable as it always was, has become difficult, and, in some opinions, foolish. By a dangerous extension of Dr. Johnson's remark on Dryden's preface to the " Maiden Queen " that " what is good only because it pleases, cannot be pronounced good till it has been found to please," it is now often proclaimed that what immediately pleases only a small number of readers must necessarily be inferior to what immediately delights a crowd.

It may be that these observations might strike a foreign critic as being based on just that insularity of view which is typically English. Certainly, the gulf between taste and life—these terms are used simply as convenient shorthand symbols—has, in a sense, not become so portentously enlarged in countries like France and Italy. If their languages have exact equivalents for " highbrow," at least they are not so frequently bandied about in periodical criticism ; and the proportion of purely popular literature to conscientious works of art is much smaller than it is in England or America. Further, such " best-sellers " as there are depend, in comparison with Anglo-Saxon ones, far less

upon adventure, varied incident, mere sequence
of exciting events and details of social conditions sentimentally treated : though their
situations are more stereotyped they are less
obsessed with the modern journalistic fetish
of a good " story," and they can always reckon
on the perennial spring of strong emotions which
ideas start from Latin minds. On the other
hand, these writers have not inherited, and are
not forced to take into account, the passionate
restlessness and thirst for experience of the
Anglo-Saxon. The name of the Spanish
novelist Ibañez might be quoted in contradic-
tion of this : but it might then be retorted
that Ibañez, who began as a Spanish novelist,
long ago became an international " best-
seller," formed as much by American demand
as by any other influence. It would be more to
the point to object that from Victor Hugo
onwards the novel of life and adventure has
flourished in France, with Loti, About,
Merrimée, Claude Farrère, and now Benoît's
"Atlantide" and the lively but disillusioned
movement of Morand's " Ouvert la Nuit."
Yet, were there space, much might be said
to minimise the weight of any comparison
between this French school and what Anglo-
Saxon publishers mean by stories with a

" punch " in them. The intellectualism of Morand's clever tales, for example, with all their brilliant cosmopolitan colouring, is really on a level with a novel like Cocteau's " Le Grand Ecart," which, to the average Englishman, would be quite unintelligible, though it is written with the utmost clarity. However, notwithstanding a distinct romantic bent in some French minds and, in particular, their passionate interest in the East, the literature which it has produced bears but a small proportion to the bulk of French literature. As for the Italians, with the possible exception of Manzoni's " I Promessi Sposi," they have, to their own regret, been unable to produce the fiction of glamorous adventure or even of romantic realism since the days of the *novellieri* and of the heroic poetry which ended with Tasso. They read our Richardson, Fielding, Kipling and Wells with an intense admiration for the swiftness and liveliness of their moving pictures of life : but, of their own, they can only offer the luscious eloquence of D'Annunzio, the philosophical and witty irony of Pirandello, the passionate peasant life of Deledda and the warm geyser of Guido da Verona's emotion. Criticism, too, in Latin countries, though often facile and sometimes

venal, is invariably conducted on an artistic
level, and the frank acceptance of commercial
standards, which distinguishes the critical
attitude of the English and American popular
press, finds small place in it.

On the other hand, it is unlikely that intelligent continental critics regard the state of
literary taste in their own countries with undue
complacency, for there is a reverse side to the
picture. This, bluntly stated, is that only in
Anglo-Saxon countries is reading a truly
national pastime. Even in Germany, where
the standard of general education is extremely
high, and certainly in France, where the
language is so thoroughly taught and so proudly
cherished, the output of literature with a
popular appeal is small in comparison with that
of England and America. In other European
nations—though I speak with diffidence of
Scandinavian countries—it is smaller still.
Every English traveller, knows for example,
the dingy scantiness of the continental press,
though he may not take the trouble to observe
its usually high propriety of expression. No
Englishman or American accustomed to the
clear arrangement, the headlines, the magazine
pages, the correspondence columns, the repre-
sentation of multitudinous interests and the

liberal supplements of his national press, would think of investing even a penny in such productions. And if he looked for the weeklies and monthlies which furnish his mental provender, the chats, the snippets, the motoring and gardening journals and, above all, the monthly flood of periodical fiction, he would not find it on the continent. To some extent, it is true, he would find analogies to the cheap reprints of ancient and modern literature which are so remarkable a sign of present-day English publishing, but with a range of selection not nearly so large, because, over a large part of Europe, the buying of a book is an action almost beyond the stretch of imagination. Italy is anything but a benighted country, yet the Italian publishers, at this moment, are conducting a strenuous but despairing campaign to overcome what they call " the book crisis." In the propaganda of this campaign there have been envious references to the universality in England of that common piece of furniture the bookshelf. Apparently bookshelves are rare in Italy, and an Italian business man has been heard to say that, in his opinion, to spend a shilling on a book is a waste of money. These things are recorded, from Italian sources, in no spirit of censure, but only to make clear the fact that, for a variety of sociological reasons, the great public in a country like Italy, one of the predominant nations, has not arrived at the enormous and still increasing literary development of the great Anglo-Saxon public. They will reach it in time, as they will in other continental countries : meanwhile, when this is recognised, it does not appear so wonderful that literary taste seems purer than ours and less in conflict with the unchastened desires of a vast number of hurried but voracious readers. That vast public has yet to grow, and to become, through its influence on art and criticism, the disturbing element that it has become in England and America. It *will* grow, and the pellucid waters of even Latin taste *will* be disturbed : its leaders will then see that a universal demand for literature of some kind brings its own drawbacks and perplexities in its train. In England of to-day these drawbacks and perplexities are obvious ; yet the honest observer, though he may deplore the temporary carrying away of aesthetic landmarks, must admit that our flood of reading matter is a better and healthier thing than the neater but more restricted canalisation of other countries.

It is vital to the strong growth of English letters, at all events, that the English critic, while fully recognising the conflicting elements in the present situation, should be this honest observer and rejoice, in the strength of his own love for literature, that what is written in the English tongue reaches freely so vast a multitude, with its infinite degrees of understanding and varieties of temperament. Although in a very limited and particular sense Mr. T. S. Eliot's hard saying may be true that " the moment an idea has been transformed from its pure state in order that it may become comprehensible to inferior intelligences it has lost contact with art," it is a truth of small practical value : nor is it a good general statement, for art is a special channel of mental activity, whereas intelligence is a faculty of universal application. Who, indeed, is justified in calling any intelligence inferior till he has tested it upon all levels ? Art is only one among many human functions, though, at its highest, it may give supreme significance to all the rest ; so it is wiser to recognise that those to whom, at any moment, only lower degrees of imaginative creation appeal are, nevertheless, a potential field for the most precious seed. On the other hand, it is foolish and harmful to proclaim

that the immediate enjoyment of the greatest
numbers is a final test of value, that taste is
a worthless idiosyncrasy, and that the higher
sensibility which invariably grows from the
study and analysis of great works of art is a
possession of no account. Since commercial
standards rule so much of human action at
present, it is not surprising to find this view
frequently asserted or tacitly assumed ; but
its absolute acceptance would mean the death
of art more certainly than the dictation of the
most decadent eclecticism. The artistic
impulse could shake off the latter in a generation, but the stranglehold of the former might
last for centuries. However, neither the conscience of the creative writer nor the casual
opinion of those who only respect present
success is here in question : it is the attitude
of the critic. The critic's difficulty is to keep
his mind free from cant and his vision single ;
he has to form his judgments between the
opposing inhibitions of the artistic sensibility
which he has laboured to cultivate, on the one
hand, and, on the other, his fear of proving
himself pedantically near-sighted. It is hard
to find in the works of our leading critics any
clear solution of this problem, save that certain
of them succeed in dealing out the sound

judgments of a trained appreciation in a
form that is attractive to many and diverse
minds. But neither the moral " humanism "
of Mr. Middleton Murry, nor Mr. Eliot's
" seriousness " nor the transcendentalism of
Mr. Fausset nor the technical approach of
Mr. Percy Lubbock set an infallible course for
the critic of to-day who, without being either
rigidly aloof or ridiculously expansive, would
equip himself to meet the wonderful diversity
of modern literature with uniform justice,
tolerance and acumen.

No single formula, it is true, is likely to meet
the case, since it has to be realised that there is
no such thing as a standard reaction to a work
of art. A mind, for instance, which finds in
Mr. Hardy's " Dynasts " a noble and moving
picture of great action might consider a
narrative like Mr. Sinclair Lewis' " Main
Street," or Mr. Hutchinson's " If Winter
Comes " unimportant, possibly false ; yet
other minds—not necessarily inferior in human
value—might find a true poetic significance
in the vicissitudes of Mr. Sinclair Lewis'
heroine or Mr. Hutchinson's Mark Sabre
which they would fail to descry in Mr. Hardy's
mighty canvas of the Napoleonic generation.
So that, whatever just criticism might be

directed against the two novels, even to the extent of saying that there was little beauty in them, it could not be denied that for thousands they had fulfilled a genuinely artistic function. This kind of contrast might be multiplied indefinitely, with charges of pedantry and coterie-ism on the one side and of commercialism and vulgarity on the other; but the point is that in every case the critic will find himself with a personal predisposition to be weighed against the external perceptions of his professionally critical eye. To take one point alone, too often considered a negligible one: every day he will find what Dryden happily called the " proprieties and delicacies " of the English language violated, for, while the French still keep their bright jewel undimmed, only a few seem to care in what ragged garments our poor Cinderella of a tongue goes out in public. A few critics cannot stop the deterioration of a language or enforce a lost sense of style; but each must decide whether he is not bound to call attention to it and how far—when this question arises—he should condone the abandonment of tradition in new imaginative interests. The question of language is only one of many which arise daily in critical practice. An aristocracy of

taste no longer holds sway or sits as a court
of appeal. The critic of to-day pleads before
a huge popular assembly, and he has to make
up his mind how and to what end he shall
frame his pleadings.

It is a testimony to Mr. Eliot's critical
acumen that the temptation to quote his
incisive remarks is frequent. There are two
in his book, " The Sacred Wood," which are
suggestive in this matter. He says in one
place : " The important critic is the person
who is absorbed in the present problems of
art, and who wishes to bring the forces of the
past to bear upon the solution of these problems." It would have been useful if he could
have expanded this remark with reference to
the present and the future, showing, for
instance, how the forces of the past are to be
brought to bear on this problem of the
divergence between the art of the few and the
art of the many, especially as illustrated in the
multiformity of stories and novels, in the decay
of the nobler styles of poetry and in the dis-
appearance of high tragedy from the stage.
Mr. Eliot says again, that it is part of the
business of a good critic to preserve tradition,
where a good tradition exists. But how
is this to be done when a tradition is rejected,

215

on one side, by the large public as no longer
satisfying, and, on the other, is ruthlessly
transformed by innovators on the ground of
its being too cramped for modern imaginations ?
And what is a critic to say when an artist like
Mr. J. D. Beresford prefaces a collection of
short stories by explaining to other writers
by what artifices any intelligent teller of stories
can reap the shekels offered by American editors
to those who accept their canons ?   He can
only say that as a trade communication it is
interesting, but that with the art of fiction it
has little to do.   Mr. Beresford lost his opportunity of saying something far more valuable,
which would have put the by no means
negligible demand of the market in its proper
place while pointing out the line of victory
for disinterested art.   He should have said,
what perhaps he meant to say, that in a form
now so chaotically used and so continuously
debased as the short story, the high hope of
the future lay, not in the dragging down
of fine art to the level of commercial craftsmanship, but in the determination of fine
artists to raise the common to their level.
And this is the truth that Mr. T. S. Eliot
perceived when he suggested that the one hope
of reviving the poetic drama would be to inspire

a truly popular form of entertainment, such as the music-hall turn, with some poetic germ which might develop into a form of art as vital and as genuinely national as the drama of the Elizabethans.

It is, surely, to some such idea as this that the fastidious critic must cling, now and for the future, in his frequent bewilderments, not the least of which is that fastidiousness itself seems often to be regarded as a crime, whereas it is an inevitable accompaniment of greater understanding. He is bound to insist that in the consideration of all art the ultimate standard must be high, completely attainable by few, and must include the great and the supremely beautiful in all ages of literature. To suppose that new social conditions, new phases of interest and the demands of a new public can effect or warrant any break in the tradition of art is a false and unworthy notion : and if a critic cannot honestly reconcile his judgments of the present with every stage in his knowledge of the past, he deserves no confidence. On the other hand, it is upon his understanding, not upon his fastidiousness, that he will pride himself ; and not upon understanding alone, but upon his determination to direct it without stint on the problems

of his age. It is easy enough for a critic to
treat the past alone with veneration and deal
indifferently with the present, or to live aloof
in the conventicles of to-day while sneering
at the mass-meetings : but if he will not take
all things into account, he will be of little use
and no importance. And, though it is the
artist, not the critic, who brings about the
great revolutions, the critic cannot exercise
his understanding more fruitfully than by
scrutinising the work of the present for the
promise of the future, fostering the germ of
living art in whatsoever humble or strange
surroundings he may find it, and unequivocally
denouncing what is dead matter, though a
writer of consequence should put it forth.
Engaged in this activity, like a prospector
for gold patiently washing an illimitable but
poor alluvial deposit, he will find his task tedious
and exacting : and he will often groan at the
hours consumed in sifting journeyman-
literature when he might be fortifying himself
with the work of masters. Yet he who neither
throws up the business in disgust nor abandons
it in despair need not fear that his self-denying
labour will be thrown away. At the present
moment more than ever the vast community
of readers needs the guidance of discriminating

minds, who, both in introducing to them the masterpieces of the past and in commenting wisely upon the present, can make art a live thing and plain truth clearly intelligible. The virtues of contemporary literature are energy, indefatigable curiosity, an interest which sweeps its net wide over all the activities of mankind, and a passionate determination to take all life, in every gradation, for its field and to find therein the great but simple issues. Its faults are a careless expansiveness, a certain artistic aimlessness, an immense satisfaction with unimportant detail, a complacent shapelessness, a crude emotionalism and—as a reaction against this—a kind of boisterous cynicism. It is the business of the critic to separate the virtues and the faults in every instance, praising with enthusiasm, castigating without fear, and never ceasing to put men in mind of the highest in each kind—of poetry that transcends the chirpy lyric, of essays more polished than the conversation of the smoking-room, and of drama, whether in play or novel, more significant than the casual reportings, criminal and domestic, which furnish an hour's desultory reading for the idle.

The best of our contemporary critics justly estimate and courageously endeavour to carry out their task. They are not pedantic or coldly supercilious ; they do not express themselves in aesthetic jargon nor are they captious in faultfinding : indeed, they praise too freely and castigate far too sparingly. Too often there is silence where sharp criticism would be salutary. Their attitude—and Mr. Robert Lynd most freely admits it—is that a critic, conscious of his own human imperfections, had best keep his pen for giving thanks, for occasionally censuring the wholly pernicious and for reproving the backslidings of the elect. I suggest that it is also the critics' duty to stigmatise the feeble, the commonplace and the false when possible, and that the public would thank them for doing so in a manner which fairly and simply exhibited the grounds for this correction of taste. They may reply, with truth, that within the limits of a short review or article it is impossible to contain a reasoned argument and that adverse criticism, if it appear arbitrary, is both ungrateful and ineffectual. ' Certainly, unrelated spasms of condensed censure will do no good : but criticism is not entirely conducted in short spaces, and it is in their books and longer studies that the critics might be more ready to perform the function of touchstones. One reason why English criticism too often appears incomplete and inconclusive is the omission on the part of its authors to relate their knowledge of the past to their perception of the present : they tend to regard new works and contemporary writers as isolated phenomena, relating them neither to their own nor to preceding ages. Too seldom do they attempt to put themselves in the position of a critic of the future to whom, for instance, the work of a Conrad, a Galsworthy, a Bennett or a Lawrence will appear, not as a particular growth of a particular temperament, but as a term in the long series which begins with Fielding, Richardson and Smollett. From such a point of view, which can be made implicit without detailed elaboration, the merits and faults of contemporary writers are seen in a just perspective and the examination of them may be made a useful and persuasive education of public taste.

In a word, English criticism might pay more attention to its background, for it is in this respect that it can with greatest certainty assist the casual reader. A man or woman who has read a book with pleasure or distaste of a certain kind may reasonably refuse to be persuaded by a bare assertion that these feelings

were unjustified : but if it can be revealed
that they have been enjoying the lower through
ignorance of the higher or have overlooked
beauty which a sensibility cultivated by profitable reading would have observed, such persons
will be tempted to acquire the knowledge that
will mend their judgments.   It is here that
there is virtue in Mr. T. S. Eliot's insistence
on the critic's paramount duty of elucidation
—of making, that is, the elements of judgment
so clear that the conclusions are, as nearly as
possible, inevitable.   But he goes too far in
wishing to eliminate all expression of opinion.
The discussion of art can never be similar to
mathematical analysis :   the   absolute   and
ultimate truth about it can only be a precious
residue filtered through the best opinion of
many ages.   The creation of a background
is in itself, in the last resort, opinion, though
it can be opinion very strongly propped by
accepted facts.   Recently   the   methods   of
critical biography adopted so strikingly by
Mr. Lytton Strachey and Mr. Nicholson have
admirably illustrated the advantage of careful
structure in criticism.   Half the clarity and
the truth, more than half the delight, which
are to be found in the former's " Queen
Victoria " and in the latter's " Byron : The

Last Phase " depend upon their author's exhaustive preparation of a background which, in the works themselves, is painted in with a rapid certainty and a deft economy. The figures stand out solidly against this background in well-defined relations, and the effect of illumination was so remarkable that a story which all the world thought it knew was, in each case, made fresh to it.

Illumination is but a synonym for good criticism. Confusion vanishes in a clear light, and the only light in these matters is the light of knowledge skilfully applied. Moreover, as Mr. Middleton Murry is rightly never tired of insisting, the critic's knowledge must not be only of printed books and facts, but also of the soul. The sincerity and sensibility of our contemporary critics is not to be questioned, but the confusion of contemporary letters can only be cleared up and the conflicting standards of appreciation only reconciled by regarding new works of art in just perspective against the background, not under the shadow, of the past. Presented thus, given significance and proportion, the braveries of great artists and the pettinesses of imperfect ones will be clearly discernible by all who have common understanding. Genuine art has nothing to fear from such a process, though it may reduce to puny stature some puffed-out heroes of popular vogue. And thoroughness in criticism alone will spread the knowledge and foster the sensibility which, as the love of English letters spreads still wider and burns brighter, will enable the mighty host of readers to re-echo with intenser conviction and ever growing unanimity of reference the thankful cry of Coleridge : " What great men hast thou not produced, England, my country ! "